To: Sandra

AFTER
the
FALL

my journey to freedom
from communism to capitalism

GABRIELA GERHART

enjoy the read!

Gaena

ISBN 978-1-7355883-8-4 (Hardcover)
ISBN 978-1-7355883-6-0 (Softcover)
ISBN 978-1-7355883-7-7 (eBook)

Printed in the United States of America

Published by Publish & GO Press—Houston, Texas
www.publishandgo.com

PUBLISH & GO PRESS

H O U S T O N

Table of Contents

Dedication

_____

To my parents, for your love, selflessness and
instilling great morals in me.

To my husband, Gary, for your love, care, and true
partnership on this adventurous journey.

To my American friends, clients and family,
for your warm welcome and support.

Preface

This year marks the 22nd birthday I have celebrated in America—exactly half of my life split between two worlds. The first half living under communism and it's lasting effects, the second half living under capitalism. I have experienced complete opposite ends of the socioeconomic spectrum in a way not many people can say they have. I do not regret either for they have made me who I am today, although given a choice, it would be no contest.

I am a woman who likes simplicity. I like being grounded; however, I crave change, spontaneity, and adventure. I have a great passion to learn and explore the world.

When I was a young girl, I remember looking forward to being 40 years old. I thought, "When I'm 40, I will be mature and wise, and people will respect me and my opinions. Yet at the same time, I will have much of my life ahead of me." On my 40th birthday, I had this question in my heart, "Have I arrived?" Am I this person I dreamed I would be?"

Have you ever asked yourself the same question, wondering "Who am I?" It seems a lot of us have.

Covid-19 has certainly shaken our confidence as individuals and as a nation. It's made travel more difficult, as well as visiting friends, or giving hugs, or even sharing a smile. These are very emotional times for the whole world. Yet, in the midst of it all, I felt compelled to write a book. Yes, this Czech girl who could barely speak any English when she arrived in America in 1998, wrote a book. With an accent!

What is the book about?

This book is about choices in life, celebrating success, celebrating history and heritage, moving on after betrayal, falling down, getting up, and opening up emotions that have been suppressed out of self-preservation, or maybe for reasons unknown. This book is about freedom—freedom to explore, to be yourself, to live and to love.

On the surface, this book is about me growing up in a communist country, and later exploring democracy and freedom—my life before and after the fall of communism, and before and after falling in love, traveling the world, and starting a business.

But beyond that, this book is about all of us—the core drive of humankind to explore and seek adventure, truth, and freedom and to get back up after any type of fall in life and to keep moving forward.

A while back, my husband planned a trip for us, to travel to an island near Honduras called Roatan. What a great time we had, staying in a delightful beach apartment just footsteps from the beach. Crystal blue water and a deep diving spot visited by many people from all over the world was just a hundred feet away from us. It was an idealistic trip. We explored the island, played golf, snorkeled, swam, and fished.

One day while exploring this relatively small island, we noticed a sign as we were driving. The sign said, "Czech Village to the right." Czech Village? We were on an island in the middle of nowhere. Was that for real? Is that some type of a joke or a surprise my husband did for me? He would do those types of things, so it would not surprise me. However, he was as surprised as I was. We both were really shocked. As avid explorers, we of course turned around and followed the sign. After a few minutes of driving, we arrived in the Czech Village. I was totally confused. The homes, the ladies walking by our car speaking Czech, and dressed Czech, then there was a Czech beer pub. My brain was totally confused. What is this? What is this all about. Why is there a Czech village in the middle of the island of Honduras? Such an exotic place for Czech people to make their home.

In a way, that experience was one of the first seeds for me to start thinking about writing a book. I of course shared my experience with my family back home, and everyone was in disbelief. No one could understand how the Czech Village appeared in Honduras. After I investigated more, I learned that this Czech Village was created by Czechs who left the country soon after the fall of communism and started investing in those properties and started businesses there. One of the first being a brewery. Naturally Czechs wouldn't live without their beer, and orchards, and farms.

But as I thought about this, I thought about the drive in the human spirit to explore, to be self-sustained, to find adventure and ultimately to seek freedom. This is what drove me to America as well when I was just a young woman out of college. I wanted adventure. I wanted to explore the world. I wanted to see what opportunities were open before me. I wanted to live and be free and create a life of my own choosing. And I have. From the outside, people might say my life has been a fairytale, a real-life Cinderella story, if you will. From the inside, I know my life was shaped by risk, passion, determination, drive, and hope; a pioneering spirit that would never give up.

Maybe you've had a "fall" of your own that you are moving on from. As you read my story, my hope is that you too will be stirred and inspired to go after the life you want—to get back up, to be willing to evolve and grow and pioneer your dreams. More than anything, I hope it inspires within you a drive to seek and stand for the precious freedom to do all of these things and to always know there is a beautiful life ahead, after the fall.

CHAPTER ONE

The Drip

To this day, the sound of running water drives me crazy. It may seem silly to some, but anytime I hear the gushing of the faucet while someone is waiting for the hot water to come in, I have a visceral response. I don't know if I will ever get over it. I won't even let my friends do the dishes at my house. I often think about how the things we've observed, felt, and experienced during childhood impact the way we feel and respond to life as adults. I believe our experiences as children certainly shape us and stay with us all throughout life.

My upbringing was very different from those around me today. I was born in a small village in the mountains of Czechoslovakia in the 1970's. Our family didn't have much, but I never felt deprived. There was no looking around and comparing what we had with what other kids at school had. There was no "hot" new toy advertised that we secretly wished for.

Everyone around us basically had the same thing. We were all in the same economic situation and had the same standard of living, and pretty much all the same belongings. At the store, there weren't a lot of choices of anything—maybe two or three options for a winter jacket and everyone wore the same shoes, pants, shirts, and sweaters. Everyone cooked at home, but we always had food on the table. Our basic needs were met. Needless to say, we lived pretty simply. We had a multi-generational home, like most. Both of my parents worked full-time, so my grandma would help us get ready for school, and then after school, she would make snacks and supervise us until evening when my parents returned. I'm thankful that we always had family around, cousins, aunts and uncles were all nearby. It was a loving and nurturing upbringing. I had no idea my family was facing such hardship, nor did I understand the oppression we were under.

There was a lot we didn't talk about growing up. It seemed there were secrets. There was so much I didn't understand until much later in life—like why we had a large Jewish cemetery in our town when no Jewish people ever lived there. Our village was small, and we passed by it often so it's not like we just forgot about it. We just knew not to talk about it. We also never spoke about politics. No one dared express an opinion that might be against the regime. They were listening at all times and if you disagreed with the party, there was a penalty to pay. For your entire family. My parents knew this all too well and complied strictly.

You never knew who you could trust or who was a spy for the communist party. There were "snitches" for the government everywhere. You never knew if the lady pushing the baby buggy in the park was a spy, or your neighbor, or even someone in your family. As an adult I learned there were over 70,000 commissioned spies in our small country of less than ten million. That's about one spy for every 150 people.

One time my grandpa, who was always a loving and kind person, was caught illegally listening to the BBC on his secret radio in his own basement. The BBC was one of the only uncensored radio station that he could get on his illegal short-wave radio. Every other radio station, and all TV stations and all newspapers were censored by the Communist Party, so you never heard the truth or knew what was happening in the world outside of what the government wanted you to know. You were only allowed to hear, see, and read what the government approved of. It was hard to know what was real or not. But one night, the neighbor saw the light on in my grandfather's basement and peered through the window to see him listening illegally to the radio. The next day, my grandfather was demoted on his job.

It wasn't always this way. In 1968, when my mom was a young teen, she observed the occupation by the Soviet Union not even knowing what was happening. She, her brother, and many of their other friends were on a train heading to Prague to find jobs for the summer. By the time they got to their destination after about a five hour train ride, the occupation invasion was already underway. As my mom, her brother and their friends were exiting the train station in Prague they could see the Russian tanks rolling in. None of them had any idea of what was happening. They had seen tanks along the train ride at one point and waved at them, thinking they were setting up for some kind of parade. It was no parade. It was a sudden takeover of Czechoslovakia by the Soviet Union. Over 2,000 tanks and 200,000 Warsaw Pact troops with 800 aircrafts invaded our humble country. My mom and her friends were quickly redirected to a safe place away from the tanks that were destroying property and hurting people as they rolled down the streets of the city. My mom recalls collecting a few of the flyers that were swirling in the air during all of the chaos. She later learned how thankful my grandpa was for them, as they were flyers that contained the truth; anti-communist propaganda. He was so nervous to have them in his possession in their home, as it would turn out badly if they were to be discovered during one of the random visits and searches conducted by the regime and secret police.

The radio station in Prague was the first destination for the tanks and the troops to target. They were trying to stop the news from reporting what was actually happening in Prague so they could prevent awareness from spreading to neighboring towns and cities. The first step in the takeover was preventing freedom of speech. During the invasion, about 70 civilians were killed trying to stop the tanks. This all happened in a matter of hours. It's amazing how freedom and democracy is so fragile. Our country had been under the Communist Regime since 1948, but our country was given to Russia after World War II, and things definitely intensified after the summer of 1968.

Strict allegiance to the Communist party was coerced. Often people were put in the position to either follow an order or lose their job, and therefore lose the ability to provide for their families. Anyone who wanted to have a good, or just a decent job needed to join the Communist Party. If you wanted to get any type of professional degree, or higher education, you would need to join the Communist Party. If you didn't do well in school, you would be placed in a "special" school—something to be avoided at all costs.

To prove you were a good communist and supportive of the regime, each person would carry a red book and on an annual basis, purchase a star sticker to place in your red book, which you would keep at your home or on your person in case it was asked for.

Needless to say, my entire life my parents were very careful about all of their activities and what they would say or not say, especially in front of the children. What a child hears at home, they take to school and many of the teachers were part of the communist movement and had no problem reporting a family to the authorities. Controlling the education system was also a key to promoting Communism. In general, people were very careful in pubs, and never drank too much so that they wouldn't talk too much or say anything they would regret. You never knew who was listening. Of course, being so young, I had no idea about any of this.

I was okay with the fact that our family didn't talk much about current events. It had become a way of life. I didn't ask many questions, but there was something my mother did on a regular basis that really piqued my curiosity. Every few days, she would reach on top of the kitchen cabinet and pull down a calendar that she stored up there. She would review it and write on it and then return it to the top of the cabinet. Who keeps a small calendar on top of the cabinet and why? I wondered. I had to find out. One day without her knowing, I climbed up onto the kitchen counter to see what she had been writing. As I looked over the calendar, what I saw made me realize how very poor we were. On it, my mother was keeping notes about money she would borrow from my aunt and my grandmother. She needed help just to get by. She would log when she got the money and when she would pay it back, either the next week or the next month, tracking every penny and keeping it all in order. As I looked at that calendar, I began to understand that my family was barely making it, living paycheck to paycheck.

My parents survived by living frugally. They would always walk around the house turning off lights or unplugging electrical appliances when not in use. They were also extremely conscientious about saving water—anything to stretch those precious Czech Korunas, our money. We would take baths–never showers–with just a few inches of water, reusing every drop and never leaving the faucet on for any reason. It seemed like a sin to do so. I felt like I was doing my part as I helped to conserve our resources. Trying to keep my mere existence from being a financial burden on my parents was a huge responsibility as a young girl, one that I never grew out of. I'm reminded not to be a burden every time I hear the faucet drip.

Thankfully, we lived in the countryside where we raised animals, grew our own fruits and veggies, and made our own canned preserves out of strawberries, cherries, pears, or apples. We would also help my parents by working in our yard, cutting grass, picking produce, or harvesting potatoes. In the evening we would build a fire behind the house and grill sausages on a stick. We would then bury fresh dug potatoes or freshly picked apples in the coals and let them cook for a while before eating them. It all tasted so amazing—fresh and flavorful! We picked lots of berries, raspberries, blueberries and blackberries in the forest gathering them for my mom or grandma to make our baked goodies, homemade pies and tartlets. We also made canned pepper or cauliflower pickles, relish and sauces, and we had boxes and boxes of potatoes and carrots, plus canned apples, cabbage, and sauerkraut barrels stored in the basement for winter. We always had food and we would trade what we had with the neighbors in exchange for forest mushrooms, meat, milk, eggs, hay, or some other harvest. Our community relied on one another. We had to.

This was such a sharp contrast to what it was like for kids growing up in America in the 1980's—a free country. There was no need for a family to store up food for the winter in order to survive, and the retail stores certainly had more than one or two choices for a winter coat. Our country was only allowed to trade with other communist countries, so we never even saw anything from America. The government wouldn't risk influence from a free nation.

Growing up in communism, and not having extra money or access to many things meant that by default, you would learn how to make things from scratch. Everyone developed a skill to create things. Even building a home. There were no construction companies to hire or mortgage loans to apply for. You would borrow money from family and friends and start building your home yourself once you saved up enough money for the raw materials. When you had the materials, you would ask your friends and family members to come and help you. Most of the time it took a long time before you finished the house because of the lack of resources, or because you couldn't find enough hands to help. But in general, everyone tried their best to be there for each other and help each other out. And everyone would reciprocate the help for other's projects.

Soviet indoctrination started early in life. The drip of propaganda started when I was just six years old, which was the time to join the Socialistic Youth Union created by the Communist Party. It initially started innocently, like the Scouts program in America. We had regular meetings in our starched uniforms, wearing blue button-down shirts and a red neckerchief, neatly tied—which took a lot of practice. We would rehearse certain poems, take oaths, and memorize mission statements on how to be a "good Pioneer." We were taught how to participate in the building of socialism through discipline and hard work. We were trained to be loyal and serious comrades, conforming to the will of the collective which was the highest priority. We were also, of course, taught to be dutiful, always listening to our superiors, parents, and those in authority, doing good for our community. We were groomed to be compliant and rewarded for following the rules and blending in. I was always striving to be in leadership roles and ultimately the president of the class.

Communism also focused heavily on physical activities. There were many organized sport events that everyone was required to attend. Everyone had to be physically active. There was an annual national gymnastic event called Spartakiada sponsored by the communist party, with tens of thousands of participants who trained all year long for this event which highlighted the strength of the young and the strength of the family unit. Synchronization of thousands of bodies showcased uniformity and the strength and power of communist youth. It was all about presenting the strength of communism to the world.

In my later elementary years, the focus on athletics drilled into us combined with my adolescent interest in boys, shaped my choices for extracurricular activities. One of the boys I had a crush on was taking judo after school, so I signed up for judo as well but after just one class, I knew it wasn't for me. Another one of my crushes had joined a train model building after-school program. I actually stayed in that program for quite a while and he helped me to build many train models and terrains. As I got older, I decided to pursue bodybuilding and developed quite a passion for it—and yes, I had another boy crush. But I also wanted to be one of the ladies on stage, showing off my strong physique. I trained hard but once I reached a certain level, I realized I would need to start taking steroids or supplements to compete with the others, so I stopped. I was also a very active volleyball player and that suited me better.

I never dared ask for anything from my parents growing up because I was so sensitive to our financial situation. My parents never talked about money in front of any of us kids, but I could feel the enormous amount of pressure they were under and carried it with me.

Part of our school winter activities was a week-long ski trip to a nearby village where all of the students from my class and other grades would gather and learn how to ski, or how to ski better. I wanted to go so badly but I knew it would be a financial strain for my parents. All the kids in the neighborhood were excited and preparing to go. My mother asked me one day, "Gabi , are you excited to go on the school trip?"

Thinking fast, I replied, "No mom, my knee is bothering me. I don't think I can even ski. It wouldn't be wise for me to go."

Mom just looked at me curiously, but she didn't push it. Knee problems run in my family so it was a very believable story. We both wanted to believe it. Even though I was sad to miss the trip, I knew my parents were already doing so much for me and I was grateful they wanted me to have the opportunity to go.

Because we didn't have a lot of material possessions, we spent a lot of time outdoors with our cousins and friends, playing ball, hide and seek, exploring the forest, riding bicycles, exploring the rivers and its banks, and exploring the beautiful land all around us. I don't remember having too much homework like the kids seem to have nowadays. In my day, we were encouraged to go outside and play.

I remember making mud pies with my sister, mashing the earth and water together, patting out a cake and setting it in the sun to dry. We really felt like we were cooking and took it very seriously! In the wintertime, we would build igloos in our backyard. My dad and my uncle, his twin brother, would shovel all the snow in the backyard into a great big pile and after a little work on it, we were able to dig tunnels inside it. It was so much fun, and we spent what seemed like hours playing and pretending the tunnels were our homes.

Since we were so secluded from the rest of the world, we didn't have electronics, or any kind of gadgets that kids played with. Instead, we built strong friendships with the other kids in our community as we explored outside in nature. Comradery was very important, and once you found someone you could trust and rely on, that relationship was golden—a treasure you didn't take lightly. The authentic friendships built on trust are everlasting. I could see that with my parents and their friends who are very close still, after 50 years of friendship. To this day, although they are not my relatives, I call my parent's friends my uncles and aunts. We treated our close friends like family because we all needed to rely on each other's support.

Another fond winter memory I have is when I would to go to my uncle's home with all of my cousins. He had a sauna in the basement, which was not common at all, and in fact, I actually don't know anyone else who had a sauna in their home at that time. He also had a little pool next to the sauna, which was for cold plunges. So, all of the cousins would get into the sauna and get heated up, and then we had to choose to either do a cold plunge in the pool or run outside and roll in the snow, which is what we chose most of the time especially if it was a nice fluffy snow! Right after that cold plunge or snow roll, which usually became a snow fight, we would run back into the sauna to warm up again. (Wouldn't you?) After we did this about three or four times, we would go upstairs, put on cozy sweat-pants and warm shirts, and our aunt would be wait-ing for us with hot teas and a family movie. After the movie was over, my sister and I would walk back to my parent's home across the village. I loved those quiet winter nights, with the moon shining and guiding our way. I can still hear our steps crunching in the snow, while our puffs of breath were visible in the crisp air, and everything around us was so peaceful and quiet.

I loved the winter months which signaled the com-ing holidays, the most wonderful time of the year all over the world. During the holidays, exotic citrus fruits were imported from other Communist countries like Cuba or Vietnam. We didn't have them year-round so it was a special treat indeed! People would line up at the grocery store for hours waiting to get those tasty tangerines, a deliciously sweet fruit treasured by all. There was even a limit on how many you could buy for a family, however, because my mom and dad worked in the grocery store, we always got our share first. We never had to stand in line for tangerines or fresh bread, like everyone else. We always looked forward to that day when my parents would bring home our share of citrus fruit. I have fond memories of gathering as a family in the living room, as we each were handed our tangerine or grapefruit. We would peel it and eat it so carefully, savoring one juicy segment at time. We had no idea that in other parts of the world, you could buy as many tangerines as you wanted all year round.

Communism was an invisible burden in childhood.

CHAPTER TWO

The Fall

Under communism, when you reach the eighth grade is when you have to select your career path. Everyone was "encouraged" to have either an associate, secondary, vocational or high school degree. If you were not at a level to pursue one of those, you would go to a "special" school. This is where people with learning differences would end up and you never really saw them after that. You didn't see people with special needs in society because having special needs was perceived as weakness and didn't fit the image of communism. Of course, your options for a career path depended on your grades and the demand the country had for certain jobs. You couldn't just choose whatever you wanted, you had to choose from what was available. Most of the options were "blue collar" types of jobs. There was really only the working class and the political elite, certainly no entrepreneurs.

Nothing in between. However, deciding early on about your future and going for it forced you to grow up and mature much faster than kids in other parts of the world, I'm sure.

When I entered the eighth grade, I was pretty excited about everything. I was bright-eyed and ambitious with all kinds of ideas about my future—from wanting to be a teacher because I like children, to wanting to be a police officer or an "army" girl or even a detective—which was a short-lived notion because the idea of investigating a crime scene in the middle of the night scared me. I finally settled on being a pediatric nurse. I guess because I liked uniforms as well as children and babies. At the time, the only school for pediatric nursing was about an hour and a half train ride from my hometown so that meant that I would need to stay in a dormitory during the school week. This of course was an additional expense for my parents, but they were prepared for it by this time and happily agreed for me to pursue my interest. I would finish my eighth-grade year and then head off to nursing school the following year.

I liked going to school. I had great friends and great teachers. I was always involved in school activities and after school programs. We often had projects assigned to help us learn the value of work and earning a wage.

We would collect things around town, like magazines, newspapers, paper goods, metal, and then drop them off at local collection sites where we would get a small bit of pocket money, and the satisfaction of doing good for the community. We would also collect different herbs, nettle leaves, acorns as a competition between different grades, or even different schools. The acorns were to be collected for our forest animals for the wintertime.

Another way I would earn a small bit of money is by selling rabbit skin. Our family raised rabbits and the skins were of value. I made arrangements with my dad for him to teach me how to skin them neatly so the fur would not get damaged. I would carefully turn them inside out and stretch and dry them on a special wire rack my dad created. After I had a few of them ready, I would take them to the collection site and collect my pocket money.

I mentioned that my dad was, and still is, very frugal. He was always holding on to random objects just in case they were needed in the future. My dad would collect all kinds of things: pieces of wood, wiring, metal, paper, cardboard, plastic containers, boxes, pipes, and he would always have everything anyone needed in his workshop. I used to love spending time in my dad's workshop. He was always working on something. Mom would say he was piddling. My dad, and really all of his brothers are very crafty and have the ability to build and create many things from scratch. What I realized later on in life was that developing the skill and talent to build things was not just a hobby for him or a way to pass time. Often it was a necessity because access to resources was so very limited. He learned to create whatever he needed.

My eighth grade year is easily my most memorable. But not because I was finally making money on my own or choosing my life's career path. One day in November of 1989, I sat down in my 8th grade history class like I would on any other day preparing for the lesson. But this day wasn't like any other day. This day, my whole life would change. Not only mine, but the life of everyone in the class, and in our town and in our country. Nothing could have prepared me for what was about to happen. I opened my book and pulled out my pencil as my teacher walked to the front of the room with a strange look on her face. I could have never imagined what was to come out of her mouth next. She was quiet for a moment and then very matter-of-factly, she said to us, "Well, you are all going to have to relearn history—the real history. Everything I've been teaching you is a lie. Everything you've learned about communism your entire life has been a lie."

The entire class was very confused, needless to say. I just sat there not knowing what to think, say, or even feel. I couldn't even begin to process what she was saying.

But that was the day I learned about the power of the Velvet Revolution and the fall of communism in our country. Because of the media's censorship, unbeknownst to any of us communism had fallen in Berlin just a few days prior. The communist news networks would never speak of something like this but there was an underground group of rebels that were emboldened to rise up in our country. I had no idea there was even pushback against the communist party. My parents didn't either. The movement started with students and artists in the bigger cities. Our future president after the fall of communism, Havel, was a theater writer at the time and he was jailed for many years because of his views against communism. Songwriters began an underground movement inspired by his stance and others like him. It was called the Velvet Revolution because it was through peaceful protests that things turned around. People gathered in mass, shaking keychains and waving lighters on the main square in Prague. There were no firearms or civil wars, just masses of determined people. When the people rose up, the Communists knew it was over for them.

The news of the fall was delayed since news stations were under tight control. Especially in my tiny village far away from the big city. It took a couple of days for the official word to reach my parents and their friends.

As a young, passionate and indoctrinated teenager, I wasn't very happy about all of this. In fact, I was mad. You see, I was very invested in the Pioneer movement and passionately attending meetings and climbing the leadership ladder in Communism. Now, everything I believed, supported, and strove for was all stripped from me. The most important goal I had been working towards since I was six years old disappeared. I had been taught my whole life that this was my purpose and the most important pursuit. What was to become of me? I felt lost in my own world and I was extremely upset. What or who can I possibly trust in now that my whole life, I've been living a lie? The question rang loudly in my head. The rug had been pulled out from underneath me. Everything I knew to be true was gone. It was a profound experience for a young mind.

As time went on, I began to hear stories about the other side of Communism, the dark side that was never presented to children or discussed in front of them. My older cousins and friends told me about the types of punishment they experienced when they didn't conform, or if they spoke against the regime. Their lives would be radically altered if they had a dissenting view. For example, while one of my friends who is very intelligent and on a successful career path was attending university, he was clearly a bit of a rebel and not aligned with the Communist regime. One night, he took the Russian flag from one of the buildings—a harmless college prank in most countries. However, as a consequence, he was dismissed permanently from the University and had to spend a year working in the coal mine where, at that time, only criminals were assigned to work. He had many more experiences throughout his life similar to that but he was always true to his convictions, an honorable quality by most standards. But under communism, there is no freedom of speech or freedom of expression or freedom of individuality. In my country, if you expressed a differing view by your actions, words, or writings, you certainly would stand out, and you would be scrutinized and punished.

I also heard many stories of people trying to escape the regime or flee to Western Europe. The only way to escape was to sneak across the border in the dead of night. Anyone who decided to do so could not share their plans with anyone, not even family members or they would be questioned by the authorities and punished. I cannot even imagine the dilemma, to leave your loved ones and not say goodbye. You could not even leave a letter behind because people would be questioned and punished, and phone calls would be wiretapped. If you managed to actually get to the border, you had to cross on foot and if you were detected by the guards, they were ordered to either shoot you or be shot themselves.

It was very risky to pursue freedom.

Later on, after the Velvet Revolution, archives were discovered that showed how sophisticated the monitoring and tracking systems of the Communist regime was. There were files of photographs, transcripts, and information on the general public who were being spied on by Russian informants. An innocent looking mother with a baby carriage strolling the streets would literally have a built-in camera and recording equipment capturing conversations or videotaping a meeting as she strolled around, looking for anyone resisting Communism. Or a gentleman with a very innocent looking briefcase would just pause in the streets to light a cigarette, but he was actually strategically positioning his briefcase with a camera taking pictures of the dissidents who were meeting in public or private places. We were all being watched and tracked like lab rats without our knowing. I had no idea what was happening right in front of me. I was living in a fishbowl.

As I began to understand more about what was really happening and as time went on, I started getting used to my new reality, although it took a while. The initial upside for me was that we started seeing influence from America. There was access to an influx of musical artists and as a teenager, I was drawn to rock music and concerts. But at the same time, I had a great appreciation for classical music which is something Communism instilled in us. I also developed a love for "hillbilly honky tonk" which I guess is the country girl in me. I loved all the American artists that would come and perform in our concert venues over the summer.

After my eighth-grade year, it was time to attend nursing school in Ostrava. The education was free, but my parents would have pay for the dorm since the school was in the city, an hour and a half train ride away from our village. At the tender of age of 14, I was preparing to live essentially on my own.

Ostrava was the third largest city in Czech Republic. I went from a small village in the mountains where I knew pretty much the whole town, to the big city where I knew no one. I arrived at my dorm with only a suitcase full of clothes and was greeted by our dormitory lady.

What I didn't realize is that I happened to be speaking a different dialect of the Czech language than what was spoken there and no one in the dorm understood me. It was a very difficult transition especially after my whole world was abruptly turned upside down. I would be lying if I said that I was not crying almost every day in the beginning. I didn't realize how challenging it would be to not be surrounded by people speaking my language of "ponasinu."

But soon I pulled myself together and started embracing my new life. I became friends with some of the girls in my class and learned ways to earn more money. My family gave me some pocket money to live off of, but in the big city, it did not feel like much. Of course, I didn't dare mention to my parents that I needed any more money and you know the issue there. Instead, I started taking jobs ranging from window cleaning to selling cigarettes, which were in high demand after the Communist party fell. Once we were exposed to the large variety of Western products, for some reason everyone wanted to try different brands of cigarettes. Also, banana plants and eucalyptus, interestingly enough, became wildly popular. We never had them in our country before. So, I obtained banana seeds from some young entrepreneurs in my village and then sold them to teachers and students in my dorm. There was a high demand for anything exotic and it seemed everyone wanted to start grow-ing bananas in the Czech Republic.

Even though I was starting to make an income, my views about making money were a bit distorted because of the culture of my country growing up. It was considered good to make enough money to meet your needs, but any more than that was suspicious. There was always this notion growing up that if someone had more than others, they were most likely part of the Communist party or paid off by them, or higher up in politics, or they simply stole the money. After com-munism fell, a lot of people took advantage of the vul-nerability of others and gained income and properties by taking advantage of people. So, there was corrup-tion in the wealthy both before and after Communism. Privatization was really effective for a lot of people and unfortunately it became more widely believed that if someone had a new car or a second home, or traveled or had expensive stuff, they most likely stole money from someone else or took advantage of people. As a result, many good people were scared to be wealthy and scared of abundance, not understanding that you could simply work hard to earn more; myself includ-ed. Of course, in America it's encouraged to thrive and grow and accomplish. However, it would take many years for me to give myself permission to succeed. I really had to learn to embrace success rather than be ashamed of it.

CHAPTER THREE

The Plunge

I made it to the summer of my first year in nursing school. It was all a bit of a fog with so much change happening in the world around me. But I proved to be a responsible young adult and so my parents were open to letting me travel and explore abroad. During communism, of course traveling freely was not allowed, only with permission and only to other communist countries. I remember hearing many stories of when people from Czechoslovakia would travel to East Germany or Bulgaria. Before crossing the border, they had to show a list all their belongings they had with them. There was a limit on how much cash you could bring with you as well, and of course there were no credit cards at that time. There was also a list of approved items that could be purchased abroad and brought back into Czechoslovakia. My mom shared stories with me of how people would sew extra cash inside their jacket lining or how they would find creative ways to sneak purchases back into the country. For some reason, curtains and drapery sheers were not allowed back into the country, so people would wrap them around their bodies or hide them somewhere inside the bus that was transporting the people. Some people would wear really old shoes traveling to East Germany, and then purchase new shoes and wear then back, leaving the old shoes behind. Oftentimes, a husband and wife were not allowed to travel together, because it was considered a risk of fleeing the country. They might be allowed to travel together if the children were left home with a caregiver as an incentive to return. But of course, after the fall everything was different.

In my late teens, I had my first big trip out of my home country. I was excited and broke, so I hitchhiked and went to other parts of Europe, exploring different cultures, languages, and food. I loved adventure, camping trips, kayaking, hiking and more. I'm so thankful my parents always said yes to my sometimes crazy ideas like hitchhiking through Italy or France, or taking a train across Poland, or signing up for various kayaking, mountain climbing, and camping adventures over the summers.

When I was around 16 years, I had attended one of

the most profound programs for adventurers that I had ever attended. I learned about an organization that arranged three-week long trips in the national forest surrounded by lakes and rivers. It was pretty much a camping heaven. When we arrived at the base camp, we met youth from all over the Czech Republic and Slovakia, and we were all assigned cabins. When we initially signed up for the program, we filled out a questionnaire about ourselves, our interests, and desires so we could be assigned activities during the camp. Many of the activities were focused on art, nature, or personal development. There were structured programs throughout the day and evening.

While I was excited about the idea of all of this, I didn't know anyone there. Throughout the three weeks, I had days when I was feeling very homesick. I was also one of the youngest attendees, so at times I felt a little lost, trying to understand and process all the different games we played. But I certainly enjoyed the many hiking and kayaking trips, and guitar playing by the fire at night, and making our own food while living in the wilderness. I also enjoyed the team building exercises, scavenger hunts, and so much more. One late afternoon, towards the end of the third week, we were all asked to attend a group gathering which involved role playing. We were asked to draw a ticket which would reveal a character we would be playing that evening. We were told not to share our role with others until instructed. Once we all had our assigned roles, we were invited over to a big pile of clothing and accessories so we could create a costume and dress up appropriately for our character. Some roles required nice clothing and were high-class, desirable positions, other roles were more like servants or peasants. I found clothing for my role as a photographer. I wore a light gray colored jumpsuit, trendy barrette, then found some accessories, and a fake camera. As the night went on, we were all supposed to act out our roles, and pretend we were on a big cruise ship. I wasn't sure what to make of all of this but it was fun, so I walked around pretending to take pictures and creating small talk with the better dressed people. When it was dinner time, we all had assigned seating and different food was served to people based on social status. As the night progressed, we listened to some music and danced a bit, mingling with the appropriate social class. Then suddenly we heard loud sirens going off. Of course, that was unexpected and definitely concerning. A voice came through the speakers saying there was a fire on the boat, and we needed to evacuate. I looked over to my left and could actually see smoke and flames. We all started moving in the direction we were told, which was leading us towards a dark wooded area away from our camp site. I was wearing high heel shoes with my jumpsuit, but that didn't slow me down. I was caught up in the story and driven by panic, not quite sure about what was really happening. In my mind, I knew it was part of the game, but it felt incredibly real at the same time. As we ran deeper into the forest, we could see the camp directors staged throughout the forest with lights, directing us through different obstacle courses that were set up for us. At the end of the course was the hardest challenge of all, a waist-deep pool of mud that we all had to cross. At that point, I was losing my shoes and accessories in the mud and my clothing was super heavy. After we crossed the pool of mud, there was one final challenge. Adrenaline was coursing through my body. I'd never experienced anything like this; running through the forest in the middle of the night, escaping perceived danger, uncertain about what was next. My brain could not comprehend it all very easily. The final part of this experience was when we arrived at a large cliff—the point of no return. We had to jump off the cliff into a lake and swim all the way to shore. It was pitch black except for the brightly lit rowboat in the middle of the lake in case of an emergency. I already had a great respect for the water because I almost drowned as a young child. Jumping off the cliff in the middle of the night and swimming across a lake wasn't something I could easily prepare myself for. However, being amped up on adrenaline and motivated by peer pressure, and since I had no other option, I closed my eyes and went for it. With a loud splash I plunged into the cold, refreshing lake water. After all I had endured that afternoon and evening, it was certainly an unexpected push to the edge of my comfort zone. After swimming to the shore and completing the challenge, we had a nice reward of a hot sauna to help our bodies calm down and get ready for a good night's sleep. The whole experience was very thought provoking and most definitely one I will never forget. Beyond the fun of dressing up and the thrill of the night obstacle courses, the lesson that we are all the same when the rubber meets the road, was deeply ingrained into me.

About two years later, while I was still in school, my boyfriend, Fido, and I decided to travel to the south of France. I know that sounds very romantic and exciting—and it was. Fido and I were both adventurers. We met at a local swimming pool facility where I was teaching babies how to swim part time after school. Fido was one of the lifeguards, good looking, tall, blonde and a few years older than me. But we were both pretty young and didn't have much money, so our primary mode of transportation for our adventure would be hitchhiking. We set out and made progress mainly by catching rides with 18-wheelers, sleeping in the cabin of the truck, or setting up a tent at a truck stop, or somewhere along the highway. Truckers had to follow the law which meant they could only drive a certain number of hours per day, so when they needed to stop to have a rest, we either had to rest as well, or we caught a ride with another trucker heading our direction. We met all kinds of interesting drivers; some who were a little bit intimidating, and some who were great fun to be with. Neither Fido nor I were able to speak English, just a few words, so our communication with people was a lot of hand gestures.

A few days later we finally reached our destination in Biarritz. We had been mainly eating canned food and soups, and we hadn't showered much along the way, but we were so excited although emotionally exhausted and somewhat overwhelmed by it all.

Biarritz is a beautiful, quaint town by the ocean and Fido's parents had friends who lived there. We planned to visit with them and say hello, but since he didn't really know them very well, we decided that we needed to clean up and rest first. We booked a camp site with showers, which we so desperately needed, and after a day of rest we headed into town to find the address of where his family friends lived.

I was completely mesmerized by the quaint shops, the beauty of the ocean, the beaches, and the gorgeous scenery that was so different from where I grew up. It was a tourist destination so there were plenty of little shops all around. It was an elegant seaside town, a popular resort and vacation destination ever since European royalty began visiting in the 1800's.

When we arrived at the address, the home was more beautiful than I could have imagined, and I was a little taken back by it all. I'd never seen such a magnificent home, let alone walked into one. We rang the doorbell, and we were warmly welcomed and invited in. The family spoke both French and English and since I spoke neither, we had a very broken-language conversation with a lot of smiling and nodding. Even still, we managed to have a very nice visit, and we were invited to stay for lunch with some other friends of the family. Lunch was a four-course traditional French meal with wines, cheeses and fruits, and a meat charcuterie plate. There were fresh, fragrant flowers everywhere, and pretty people with pretty clothes, in an absolutely beautiful setting. I was already so overwhelmed emotionally by the beauty of the place I was in, and the amazing food that was served, but when

Fido somehow started a conversation in French I was shocked. It was all so surreal! He was not quite sure where all that was coming from, and neither did I. At that moment, I couldn't hold my emotions in any longer and I just started crying. I simply could not hold back my feelings. Our hosts were so kind and gracious and understanding of what was going on. After lunch, we continued our visit with them in their backyard full of flowers and beautiful greenery all around. It was an idyllic day!

One of the family friends who was visiting them was from New York. He was the first American person I ever met, an older gentleman, and I believe he might have been a teacher. He was so patient with me and my very broken and limited English, and since he knew that we would be staying in the area for the next few days, he offered to teach me some English phrases. I appreciated having a few lessons with him.

Before we left, the family learned that we were staying at a nearby campsite and invited us to stay at one of their guest houses they had overlooking the beach. We were definitely not expecting that, and even though it was a hard decision to make, of course we gracefully and graciously accepted their offer. They gave us the keys and the address to the property and told us that we will see them back again for breakfast at their home.

We first had to go back to the campsite to get our tent and belongings, but we were thrilled to head up the hill to the little house where we would be staying. When we arrived, it was like a beautiful story book in a picturesque scene on the beach! I felt a whole new wave of emotion as I entered the quaint little cottage overlooking the ocean. I wanted to pinch myself to make sure it was all for real.

A couple of days later, we were invited to attend lunch with our hosts in the nearby town of Bordeaux where their business offices were located. This was a trip of many "firsts" for me and on the occasion, I would be eating something that was a first for me as well. Lunch was of course wonderful and very French with lovely wines. The main course was beef which was very confusing to me because there was red juice running from it. To my surprise, it was semi-raw steak! Growing up in communism, getting beef was rare (no pun intended) and it was usually reserved for either Sundays or holidays. It was expensive, and most certainly not something you could eat rare or semi-rare. I don't even remember much more from that day—I was just totally overwhelmed with a thought of eating bloody meat! Of course, now when I'm asked how I like my steak, I'm quick to say medium rare or rare plus.

After we spent a few days in the area, the family asked what our next plans were and since we really did not have anything specific in mind, they asked if we would be interested in spending a few days in their other home in Chamonix. It was summertime and we had no deadline for getting back, so we thought, "Why not?" I was not very good with the geography, and had no idea where that was, but my boyfriend and I were both up for more adventure. This time, instead of hitchhiking, we were provided with a car and driver to take us to Chamonix. During the drive, I was sitting in the backseat and getting increasingly car sick as time went on. I quickly learned that the road we were on was the winding road where the Tour de France took place.

We finally arrived at our destination, and again to our great surprise, a beautiful mountain cabin was awaiting us. We spent a few days in that area, surrounded by majestic mountains and then it was time to head back home. So, snapping back into reality, we hit the road and hitchhiked back to our hometown. My "Cinderella" moment was over...or perhaps just beginning.

CHAPTER FOUR

Speaking Up

After finishing four years of nursing school, I began working immediately as a pediatric nurse in a local hospital. By this time, my relationship with Fido had ended. I realized that he was still in love with his former girlfriend. I was hurt, but I knew I needed to move on, and I did so by focusing on my career. I was just 18, and enthusiastic but also nervous about my new job. This wasn't about school anymore, I was there to take care of patients.

My first day on the job, I started in the pediatric oncology unit. Many of the children were there for a few weeks at a time getting chemo treatments. It was early afternoon and we got a call that a returning patient was being brought in. We needed to set up a room to do a sternal biopsy puncture procedure which wasn't very common. I did what I needed to do to prepare for the patient but in reality, nothing could have prepared me for what happened next. As the ambulance brought the patient in, I couldn't believe my eyes. There on the stretcher was my own sister. I knew she had a rare blood disorder and I was aware she needed to receive treatments, but I never expected to see her here. I stood there in shock for a moment as the medical staff surrounded her making assessments about what her treatment should be. But I had to be a professional about it. She was my sister, but she was also my patient. They got her stabilized and she stayed at the unit for an additional two weeks before returning home. I was glad to be there for her.

As the days and weeks went by, I was learning more about my job and my "role" as the youngest staff member. There was definitely a culture to adapt to. I was impressionable and I was not going to challenge anything my superiors decided to do, even if I didn't think it was quite right. For example, we were all working the night shift and the nurses had a napping station set up in the back of the break room. We of course were not supposed to be napping, but everyone else was doing it so I also took a nap at night as well even though it didn't set right with me. But one day, our supervisor walked in and saw the napping space set up. Shee started asking questions and there was no way to deny what was happening. That experience changed me forever. When my co-workers and I were called down on this behavior, as they say in this country, I learned what it what it was like to nearly poop in my pants. I was so embarrassed and ashamed, and although I was in a junior position and could not quite control what everyone else was doing, I knew better. The fact is that I followed the herd, even when I knew it was wrong. But I told myself I would never do that again. That lesson taught me not to be afraid to stand out in the crowd, and to not be afraid to speak the truth—even to the point that it could cost your job. After that incident, the procedures for the whole unit changed and some people were also reprimanded. And as difficult as this experience was, I'm grateful that it happened to me at such a young age. And thankfully no one got hurt because of some careless behavior.

Working in the hospital was satisfying to some degree, but I didn't like that fact that I did not have much say in the patient's care. I had to just do what I was told and follow the doctor's order, but I had ideas and opinions about things. This did not sit well with my entrepreneurial free spirit. I wanted to make my own decisions about the patients, but I didn't really want to be a doctor. As I observed other professionals in the hospital, I noticed that the physical therapists were able to do this. They would meet, assess, and develop a care plan for the patients. This seemed more like something I would enjoy so back to school I went—for three more years of physical therapy school.

I enjoyed learning and was happy to be on the way to having more control over my career. During school, we had a team project where we had to explore the city in a wheelchair. This project had a profound impact on me. One of our team members was assigned to be in a wheelchair and we were supposed to take public transportation, go shop, and tour the city. We quickly realized how difficult it was to travel the city this way. There weren't accommodations to support handicap people. Sadly, we also realized that growing up we would rarely see people with disabilities on the streets. The fact is that during communism, it was something which was intentionally hidden. People with disabilities, mental or physical, were closed in homes or institutions because they didn't fit the overall narrative, that everything is great in Communism or that everyone is equal. You would hardly ever see a homeless person, if any at all. Everyone had a job, if not, they would be in jail. As time went on, I began to realize all the injustices perpetuated in the name of Communism.

All my life, I've enjoyed challenges and putting myself into uncomfortable or new situations. I was always signing up for events where I didn't know anyone and taking courses or workshops that would challenge me and push me out of my comfort zone. After all, that is how we grow and evolve. And maybe because of this, I'm also not afraid to speak up when there is something wrong, or when I see that things are not fair. Maybe that is the reason why I was sent a letter of rejection from my dormitory one summer. I was the student body president and I had stayed at that dorm for five years! But maybe I knew too much or spoke up too much? And maybe some people didn't like the fact that I spoke up? You see, it was just a few years after the fall of communism and a lot of the older people had a hard time adjusting to this new, freer way of life. The ladies operating the dormitories were the same before and after the fall. They had been part of the communist regime and still loyal to their upbringing. This particular summer, I received a letter saying that I was not welcome to come back and join the dormitory, which is where a big part of my classroom was staying. The reason given was that I didn't fold the curtains and sheets neatly and leave them on the bed as instructed at the end of the prior school year. This wasn't quite the truth and certainly not a reason to deny someone a stay in a campus dorm but there really wasn't anything I could do about it. I had to find a new dormitory in town and had to receive written permission every time I wanted to visit my classmates in their dorm rooms. None of my friends could understand why and neither could my family or teachers. But the decision was made by a couple of ladies who perhaps were still loyal to Communism or nervous to lose their positions? It was hard to tell.

CHAPTER FIVE

The Land of the Free

As I was finishing physical therapy school, I learned of a job opening at the private hospital in my hometown. My mother knew the head doctor of the hospital, so the job was mine for the taking. I understood that if I moved back home and took that job, I would be working there for the rest of my life. But before "settling down" back home, I wanted to travel and explore some more so I decided to take a year to explore the world first. The job at the hospital would be waiting for me when I got back. Six weeks later, I found myself in America.

Growing up I learned that we had relatives living in America. It was actually my mom's grandmother's relative who immigrated to America in the 1900's. My grandma was always a little bitter about it because her relative went with her husband and two younger children, but she left behind two of her older children to be cared for by the rest of the family. They wouldn't have made it out of the country with everyone. I can imagine that had to be a very difficult decision, splitting family this way. But my grandma never met her grandma. However, they did stay in touch with the family, sending letters, clothing, or money. I can't imagine the void created by their leaving. I know my grandmother's pain was retriggered at the thought of me leaving to go to America too. It made the decision more difficult for me, but I knew I would be back in a year to settle down in my hometown. At least that was the plan.

I came to America through an au pair program, which was designed for students a few years after the Velvet Revolution of 1989 and the fall of communism in the Czech Republic and throughout Europe. The au pair program was an opportunity to travel to the United States or UK, to learn English and care for American children while living in an American home. It was a twelve month program with a one month extension for traveling. Because I had a pediatric nursing background, my skill set was in high demand and I was quickly matched with a host home. Normally it could take a few months to be matched with a family but because the family had a little emergency situation, they had an immediate need for an au pair for their newborn. I was hoping to learn better English before coming to America, instead I landed just short six weeks after signing up for the program. It was a Texas couple with four children ranging in age between ten days-old and nine-years-old.

My trip to America started with my first flight from Prague to New York. I landed in JFK airport along with hundreds of other au pairs from all over the world, filled with excitement and nerves. Of course, it was quite an overwhelming experience just to be able to fly across the ocean, and then land at this huge airport, and get around with my very limited English. We were instructed to look for a sign with the au pair program written on it. We would be participating in training for the next four days, learning about the American way of life, culture, and the American family. We all got on buses and headed to the college campus which served as our base for the next four days. As I mentioned, my English was very limited, I knew some words, but I was not very good at putting full sentences together. There were three or four other girls from the Czech Republic, and their English was much better, so I stuck close to them and definitely had to rely on them. Everything was so new, so different from anything I had ever experienced before. One day, we took a little trip on a tour bus through New York City. On another afternoon, I remember being so excited to finally purchase my first real camera. As I mentioned before, my family did not have much money, but they did send me to America with some pocket money—which I quickly spent. Unfortunately, later on I learned that the camera was a fake, an imitation of the brand that I thought I was buying. Unfortunately, it did not last very long.

Staying on the college campus was very different from the dorms back home. I've never been on a campus this large, with hundreds of girls from all over the world dining together in a cafeteria. I remember pretty vividly one of the mornings when we were going through the line at the buffet to get breakfast. I was quite hungry, and I walked over to pick up some toast. I couldn't imagine why there wasn't any sourdough bread or rye bread like I was used to. Just slices of white bread, and something that looked like cheese spread, or some type of dip. Not quite knowing what it was, but looking interesting and possibly tasty, I put quite a thick layer of it on top of my bread. Once I sat down and started eating, I took a big bite of this breakfast meal and learned what this spread was. It was not any type of cheese, or interesting dip, it was peanut butter. As you most likely know, you do not put a two-inch-thick layer of peanut butter on top of your bread! Needless to say, I had a very hard time swallowing that bite, and actually could not eat peanut butter for the next 15 years after that! I had a complete aversion to peanut butter and could not understand why on earth people would eat something like this. I hoped this wasn't a foreshadowing of things to come.

My time spent in the au pair training for America built excitement and anxiety in me for the year to come. Finally, the day arrived for us to fly to our host homes. I could barely sleep the night before wondering what it would be like. But that morning, I packed my things and then the several hundred of us loaded up on buses and headed to the airport. Even after the training, I still didn't know much about America, nor did I understand really how huge it was, or how diverse each state is but in September of 1998 I landed in my new American home of Houston, Texas. My host family came to the airport to pick me up in their light blue Toyota minivan, which of course I had never even seen a minivan before. It was about an hour drive from the airport to my new American home and my eyes were wide open taking in all the sites of the city along the way. I was my host family's seventh au pair, and each year they would invite a new caregiver/student to their home. It was a great way for their children to experience different cultures, languages, clothing, and international foods. For my host family, it was a little bit like "business as usual" since they had already experienced new caregivers coming to their home, but for me it was a completely new experience.

Upon our arrival to the home, I was very surprised and somewhat perplexed by the home and location. When I spoke with the family initially on the phone back in Czech Republic, I understood that they lived on a little farm with a creek running through it, because they told me they had Chinese pigs. Now, I didn't know what a Chinese pig was, but growing up in the countryside, I assumed it was some variety of farm animal. However, due to my very broken and limited English, it appeared we had some misunderstandings. To my surprise, we arrived at a two-story home in a very traditional suburban neighborhood, just 30 minutes from bustling downtown Houston. I was very confused and wondering where the Chinese pigs were kept. Much to my surprise, I realized that their two Chinese pigs, Maggie and Jake, were not pigs at all—when two Chinese pugs came running to the door!

Because of my limited English, adjusting to my new home and life was definitely not easy. Looking back now, if someone would have told me to go to a completely foreign country and live there for a year without knowing a single person and be essentially completely on my own with strange people, I would probably be a little hesitant. But being 20-something, I was just hungry for new experiences, for exploring and traveling. So, I spent a year with this American family that I could barely communicate with and besides taking care of a ten-day old baby, I was also responsible for three other boys ages five, seven, and nine. I did everything from making breakfast, to getting them off to school, picking them back up from school, making snacks, helping with homework and getting dinner started. (Which meant grilled chicken five nights a week.) What a lesson that was!

Because of the children's ages, I was pretty much thrown into learning the language as quickly as I could. Working with baby Cooper, I quickly started reading all the baby books to him. It was good practice for me because I could read out loud, and not worry about someone laughing at me because of my accent or mispronunciations. (Not that they would, but I was very self-conscious about it.) I would read to baby Cooper all the time, and watch Baby Einstein movies with him which allowed me to start building up my vocabulary foundation.

Working with the older boys was a little trickier. I had to use a dictionary to learn what they were supposed to be learning in school so I could turn around and then help them with their homework. Anyway, it was a bit of a struggle, and one of the big challenges was of course, correctly spelling words. Nick, the seven-year-old, was my little rebel. If he misspelled a word, he had to write it 20 times, per his mom's instructions. So of course, anytime he would misspell the word, he would try to say it was my fault for pronouncing it the wrong way. But thankfully his older brother Ryan stepped up and defended my pronunciation. Debating with a couple of headstrong young boys made me very particular about my pronunciation from then on.

Another way I learned English was by watching the TV show, Friends. In my small au pair room, I had a bed, a little table, and TV. I was so happy that the family set up the TV to display subtitles so pretty much every evening after dinner, I would watch the show. I was taking in the American lifestyle of young 20-year-olds and learning their humor, which was very different from Czech humor which is much more sarcastic. As I was reading the subtitles, I had a visual and auditory learning experience which really helped me retain things. My brain got trained to see how the words are written, but not necessarily the grammar or reasons for certain sentence structures. But I learned a lot from reading the popular American book, "Little House on the Prairie." I was encountering over 20 new words on each page that I had to look up and learn. It would take me so long to read a book!

You don't realize how your ability to read a language affects everything. Even studying for a driver's license. Most of the words related to driving were completely new, and of course the dictionary became my new friend. I had a driver's license from the Czech Republic, where I drove a few times on our country roads, and my host family assumed that since I had a driver's license, I would be able to navigate Houston roads. When I first arrived, they asked me if I wanted to take my host dad, Jeff, for a ride primarily to show him my driving skills and just make sure I was ready for American driving. Well, you can only imagine how that went. I've never seen Jeff quite so nervous! They quickly signed me up for a driving course, and somehow, I managed to pass the test. Although, I still did not understand most of the language.

Even with my license, nothing could prepare me for driving on Houston freeways—the fourth largest city in America with some of the busiest highways in the country. Three times a week I would have to drive Eric to school in downtown Houston about 30 minutes away from the house and this was before smart phones or GPS. My first time to drive the route was with the kid's grandfather. I guess they thought he was going to have the most patience with me. We drove down-town and back on the multi-lane highways, HOV lanes, fast changes and side roads—nothing like the small, country roads I drove back home. But I managed to get us there and back. The second time we drove, we had Eric in the car with us. I managed again to safely get us downtown and back. When the time came for me to take Eric by myself to school, of course I was a little nervous, but it was my third time driving the same route and I had the directions written down on my notepad. I knew when to turn right, when to turn left, when to go straight; I had everything written out. Everything started out fine, but as we were approach-ing downtown Houston after 25 minutes on the multi lane freeway, along with all the commuters heading to work, I stumbled on an orange sign which read, "detour." Oh no! I hadn't planned for detour! At that point, I felt completely defeated, having no idea what to do. I don't know how I managed to make my way to Eric's school—maybe my wilderness experience back home translated to help me in the city, but somehow, I managed to get there and back out of downtown with all of its one-way streets. It was so unsettling though, that to this day, 20 plus years later, I still get a little anxious when I'm driving into downtown!

Since I had a lot of practice driving in my Ford

Explorer au pair car, I quickly became a pretty comfortable driver, and soon the family asked me to drive to College Station every other Friday to drop off their two older boys to their biological dad for the weekend. This was about an hour and a half away, but we ended up doing the exchange at the Dairy Queen about halfway, which is where I had my first experience with ice cream you can turn upside down! Who knew something like that exists? I was hooked immediately!

American food was definitely an adjustment. It was nearing the holidays where people served their annual meal traditions and I have to say, one food experience that was very surprising and perplexing for me was the sweet potato casserole. I never had eaten anything like this before, and I was completely confused. I probably had five different Thanksgiving dinners that month because the Au- pair program hosted many different gatherings, on top of celebrating Thanksgiving with my host family. Each one had a different version of the sweet potato casserole. When I first tasted sweet potato, I assumed it was supposed to be a dessert. It's sweet and I was thrown off by the pecans on top. I didn't imagine it was something you would eat with your meat. In Czech Republic, we eat savory or fermented foods with meat. But I didn't want to be rude so at every single gathering, I ate a serving and after five meals of sweet potato, I didn't want it again for another 15 years.

Another strange food I experienced when I first came to America, was with my host family at a Mexican restaurant. Of course, this Czech girl had no clue about Mexican food, and not knowing quite what to order, my host family helped me. I soon learned that I would not be a Mexican food fan. I had never tasted cilantro before and it was so strong, I just assumed that cilantro equals Mexican food. It took me about two to three years to try Mexican food again when I realized you could have it without the cilantro. Now, I'm actually quite a big fan and oddly enough, I'm even a bigger fan of cilantro. I guess some things just take a little time to adjust to.

But adjusting to Texas food was nothing like adjusting for Texas weather. In the Czech Republic, we most certainly have four very defined seasons, but not in Texas. When I first arrived to Texas it was fall and it definitely getting cooler in the Czech Republic and everyone there was preparing for winter. However, in Houston it was a very different story. That year, it was an unusually warm year, and I remember being so confused. I never experienced the amount of humidity especially in September! I remember sunbathing in the garden in November while my family back home was shoveling snow.

They say everything is bigger in Texas and for sure that goes for the insects. On one of my first calls with my parents, I shared with them that I was concerned about the household because I saw roaches. I had never seen roaches in my life and in Texas they are as big as your thumb! But I soon learned that in Texas it's not necessarily that unusual. They come looking for a cool place out of the Texas heat and it's hard to keep them away no matter what you do—but can you blame them?

I have to say, my experience with my host family was wonderful and really shaped my view of the American culture. They were very loving and caring, and really wanted me to have a great experience in America and I am grateful for that. I had weekends off and worked from 7:00 a.m. till 7:00 p.m. Monday through Friday. I spent a lot of time with baby Cooper throughout the day, helping him to reach his milestones, and because I had a pediatric nursing background, it was very natural to me. Since baby Cooper was six weeks premature, we did have a few scares with apnea the first few weeks of his life, but he quickly became a very strong baby.

My host mom and dad, Jeff and Ellen, were both busy oil and gas executives. Jeff was a very loving and caring dad to his blended family, a great dad to Cooper and Eric as well as his stepsons, Nick and Ryan. He was also the cook in the house, so I usually started dinner around 6:00 pm, and when Jeff and Ellen came home, Jeff helped finish it up. Jeff's personality was a little bit more reserved but Ellen, on the other hand, was very outgoing. She was starting a business out of the house when Cooper was born, so for three months after delivery, she and I spent a lot of time together. She worked from home setting up her new business, while still maintaining her position in oil and gas. Ellen was a self-proclaimed workaholic. I learned from her that if you wanted to accomplish something great, to have your own company and raise a family, you really need to pour your heart and soul into it because it takes a lot of hours of dedication. Ellen would spend many hours every day in her home office on calls, handling business and talking through a headset for most of the day while wearing boxer shorts and a comfy T-shirt. I had a great admiration for her and learned a lot by watching the way she conducted herself.

CHAPTER SIX

Come With Me

Through the au pair program, I met other au pairs in the area who came from Germany, Austria, Australia, Spain and all over the world. We would get together and spend the weekends exploring Houston and sharing about our experience as au pairs. One of the au pairs I met was another Czech girl, so we naturally gravitated towards each other. She was a pretty blond with a strong Czech accent, but she spoke good English, so I thought. For sure much better than mine. Her name was Sylvia and she and I spent a lot of weekends together. Her host home was in the River Oaks area which was a very prominent neighborhood close to downtown Houston. There was much more to do in her part of town than where I was. Twenty years ago, in the Houston suburbs, there was not much going on besides the dollar movie theater and one pool table at a local bar. So, it was a no-brainer to drive to town and spend the weekends with Sylvia exploring the down-town nightlife. However, the car and I had a curfew of midnight which meant I needed to leave Silvia's place by 11:30 p.m. in order to make it home on time. I never wanted to disappoint the family by being late or give them cause to worry. I appreciated that they trusted me, and of course I wanted to be well rested since my work started at 7:00 a.m. sharp with four hungry boys who needed to be ready for school.

One Wednesday night, Sylvia and I decided to go have a drink at a happening restaurant in downtown Houston. It was a tapas restaurant and bar called Sole-ro located in a charming historic building. If you aren't familiar with Spanish food, tapas is another word for appetizers or small plates. Anytime I share this story with friends, I have to be very careful about my pro-nunciation of tapas, so it does not sound anything like topless—because it was nothing of the sort! Anyway, Sylvia and I were having a drink at the bar and had a few single men gathered around us making a small talk. Clearly we looked and sounded very different from the other girls, very European. There was anoth-er gentleman sitting at the bar next to us watching all of this, and after a little while he leaned over and asked, "Excuse me ladies, where is that lovely accent from?"

Sylvia and I giggled a little bit, and I replied, "Why don't you guess?"

He obliged us with an answer, "Is it Swedish?"

Sylvia looked very Swedish, but we did let him know that was incorrect, but he should guess again. He thought for a moment and was ready with his second guess.

"Is it Czech?" He asked with a sly smile feeling proud of himself.

We were of course very surprised, "Yes!" How could he possibly know that? The man's name was Gary and we visited with him for a little bit as he continued to finish his meal. Later on, we learned that he knew we were Czech right away because he had visited Prague just the year before. After about 15 minutes, he stood up to pay his bill and as he was about to leave, he looked me straight in the eyes and said, "If you really want to enjoy your life, come with me." And with that, he turned around and started walking down the long entry hall with the barrel dome ceiling that led out of the restaurant. Sylvia and I just stood there for a moment. I remember it like it was yesterday. I looked at Sylvia and said, "Do you want to go? Let's go!" And so, we did. We quickly headed out and met up with Gary who was standing at the valet waiting for his car. He did a double take and was a bit surprised to see us. Just then the valet pulled up with his Porsche and we nervously and excitedly hopped in. We would of course never do something like this nowadays, but back then it was different. People knew how to recognize a trusting face. Gary was a perfect gentleman and appeared to be the ultimate bachelor who just liked to have fun. He was pretty familiar with the happening downtown scene. Coincidentally, one of our first stops that evening was a dance club called Prague. Gary walked us right up to the front of the line and we spent the rest of the evening, two Czech au pairs, having a great time with a complete stranger.

It was getting close to curfew time for me and so we had to go home. But before we parted ways, Gary and I exchanged phone numbers. He called me the very next day and a couple of days later, we had our first official date. I was to meet him at his home in River Oaks and we were going to have a drink there and then go to a restaurant for dinner. That night, we started talking and never even ate because we talked so long! Or maybe it was that it took so long for Gary to understand what I was trying to say, but needless to say, we had great conversation and agreed to see each other again before I had to rush off to get home by midnight.

A couple of days later, Gary reached out to me again and asked if I wanted to go away for the weekend.

Since I did have weekends off, I agreed. At that point I had been in America about four months and was feeling more comfortable in this new culture. The weekend trip was with several other couples going to the King Ranch to hunt. At that time, of course I had no idea what King Ranch was or really what hunting is all about in America. But anything "King" sounded interesting to me. Gary told me that he would pick me up at my family home on Friday late afternoon. I shared this information with my host family and later I learned that they called him to "interview" him and get a little better understanding of who he was and where we were going. I was thankful they were looking out for me. But once they were satisfied, they wanted to help make sure I was prepared for the trip. Jeff had a lot of hunting gear in a storage closet, so he told me to help myself to whatever I wanted to borrow. When Gary arrived to pick me up, I made sure I was ready. He rang the doorbell and I opened it, standing there, head to toe in hunting gear: orange vest, earpieces, overalls, boots and even goggles. Everything looked brand new, starched and never worn. Gary just looked at me grinning from ear to ear and then grabbed my bag and we walked out to the car together. Much to my surprise, we drove to a nearby private airport. I had no idea we would be flying to King Ranch or that Gary was actually a pilot with his own airplane. I learned all of this in the moment as I was boarding the plane with another couple, who was not dressed head to toe in hunting gear. That was February 1999, and I was starting to understand what Gary meant when he said, "If you want to really enjoy your life come with me." Gary loves adventure and he loves to have fun!

We flew to the King Ranch area and checked into a hotel and the next day we drove to the actual ranch to hunt with a group of about ten or twelve people including the guides and ranchers. Coming from Czech Republic, the only cactus or guns I had ever seen were in western movies, so I was taking in this whole Texas hunting experience. The other couple who flew with us were named Greg and Lissa. They were close friends of Gary's and seemed to be a little confused about why he brought this quirky girl who could speak very little English. Greg and Lissa were serious outdoor types. Greg was like the Texas version of Stephen Irwin, The Crocodile Hunter. They weren't sure how to take me but after they saw me shoot a couple of cactuses and picked up a snake we found with my bare hands, I think they approved of this Czech cowgirl!

On Saturday, after we hunted a bit, it was time to have a lunch break, so the ranchers stopped the trucks, and we all got out, and started to set up a picnic. The ranchers had food being cooked on top of the car engines while we were driving, so the women were asked to set up the picnic area, and the men were asked to clean the quail that were just shot. Of course, I did not know anyone, and barely knew Gary, but since he was my only connection there, I asked if I could join him with the men cleaning quail rather than be with the women who I could barely talk to. Of course, he invited me to join them. All the men, and me, were standing in a circle around a table as the men started cleaning the quail. Gary assumed I would just watch but I asked if I could help as well and they agreed with a chuckle. Apparently, it was not common for women to clean the quail, but I had no idea. I grabbed my first bird and defeathered it just as I had done many times back home. As a country girl, I would often clean rabbits, or turkey, or chicken so quail was not really a big deal for me. In fact, I was easily outpacing and out-cleaning everyone else there. I think they were all so surprised and impressed, they just stopped to watch me!

Without me hearing, one of them jokingly leaned over to Gary and said, "Gary, if you don't marry that woman I will divorce my wife and marry her myself!"

Needless to say, we had a great time at the ranch that weekend, and soon every weekend turned into a trip with Gary to explore various parts of Texas. Thankfully my host home was close to the airport so sometimes we would land back in Houston at 6:30 a.m. Monday morning and by 7:00 a.m., I was reporting back to work.

I loved traveling and learning but because of my limited English, I would rarely ask a question. I would mostly listen, and I always invited Gary or anyone I was speaking with to correct my English so I could learn the right way. But, in my own defense, English can be very confusing. One of the struggles I would have was trying to understand how "shrimp" means one shrimp and "shrimp" also means more than one shrimp. The same for deer. I wanted to say "shrimps" and "deers" because that made sense. Some things I guess I will never understand.

Over my first year in America, Gary and I had a lot of fun together and enjoyed many adventures. But my commitment as an au pair for a year was coming to a close. I had to start thinking about going back home to the Czech Republic and I missed my family deeply. It was hard at times not being able to have my own family around. Phone calls back then were pretty expensive, I think I paid $10 for a calling card which would allow me to speak to my family for about five minutes. I earned about $140 a week and my income was basically pocket money since my room and board were covered.

I decided to extend my Visa for one more month so Gary and I could travel and see more of America besides weekend trips around Texas. I knew I had a medical job waiting for me back home in one of the private hospitals, and the doctor agreed to keep a position open for me. I also had a party planned, coming back home after a year in America. I was getting excited to see everyone soon. But I was also excited to explore more of America with Gary.

In preparation for my return, I shipped a lot of my belongings back to Czech Republic and decided to keep just the clothes that I needed for our travels. Once I finished my commitment as an au pair and said goodbye to the host family, Gary and I started planning our month-long trip. First, we were going to fly to Florida, to see some friends, and after that fly to Las Vegas and Oregon where Gary's sisters and their families lived. After that, we would fly to California where Gary's sons lived with their mom, and then we would fly back to Houston and I would head home to Czech Republic. I couldn't wait to see the country, but also had mixed emotions about everything. I was trying not to focus on how much I would miss Gary. From the beginning, I knew it was all temporary, so I didn't let my heart get too involved, so I thought. I've always been the type to take things day-by-day, but on the third day after my au pair assignment finished, everything completely changed.

By that time, Gary had been divorced about 13 years, with no plans on ever getting married again. He was just enjoying his life and even though we had a great time together, we did not talk about the future or plans beyond our month-long trip. So, it was very strange when Gary woke up and completely out of the blue asked me point blank to marry him! I was not expecting that at all and was taken aback by his question. He explained to me that during the night he had a surreal, and very vivid dream. In his dream, he had a conversation with his mother who had passed away about a year and a half before Gary and I met. In the dream, Gary's mother said to him, "Gary, you've been looking for a buddy and friend in life. If you let Gabi go, you may never find her again. Don't let her go." Gary and his mom had a very close relationship, and as a good son, he chose to listen to his mom's advice. It was all overwhelming to me and not anything I had planned for, so I asked if I could call my parents first and talk with them. Gary promptly moved the rotary phone from the bedside table over to me, so I quickly dialed my parents. I was supposed to be home in 25 days, and here I'm calling them with this news!

"Mom, Dad. Gary asked me to marry him."

The other end of the phone was silent. My family wasn't sure what to think. I explained the whole story and finally my parents and my sister said to me, "Gabi, if you are happy, then we are happy as well." I was twenty-three years old at the time and after I hung up the phone, I turned to Gary and said, "Yes, I will marry you."

Three days later, we arranged to get married at the Justice of the Peace. Part of the rush was passion, part of it was practicality. At that point, I needed to work on my Visa and we both needed to make actual plans for the very near future. I called Hilda, my best friend at that time, a Norwegian girl who my host family introduced me to. She was so happy for us and agreed to become my maid of honor. Gary's friend, Glenn, agreed to be His best man. We all showed up at the courthouse around lunch time, with pretty much zero preparation for all the questions we would be asked by the Justice of the Peace. No other planning or rehearsing, we just went for it.

After the ceremony, we decided to all go to hotel Omni, to celebrate. As we got into the car to drive over, Gary started the engine, and the Lenny Kravitz song "American Woman" was playing on the radio and we both laughed out loud.

When we arrived at the hotel, we started calling our friends and sharing the news that we had gotten married. Most of them were shocked and surprised since they never even heard we were engaged and didn't know that was the plan. Of course, we didn't either, just three days before that. But we had a great time celebrating, and after some drinks we all went to a well-known Houston restaurant, Tony's, which used to be on Post Oak Boulevard, and we continued the celebration there.

A couple of days later, we started our three-week long "honeymoon" in our airplane across America and I met my new family for the first time. Gary did not meet my parents until five months later, after we were able to finalize my Visa situation so I could leave the country. And just like that, I was living permanently in America.

CHAPTER SEVEN

American Woman

Every year on December 23rd Gary would host a Christmas party for his friends and family. Since we didn't really have a wedding reception, we decided to combine our wedding reception with the annual Christmas party. The home was already decorated for the holidays and so we added white wedding flowers and tulle lace everywhere to make it extra special.

Of course, it was a big deal to me, not just because of the celebration but because I had never met the majority of Gary's friends and family. As I thought about what I would wear and what it would be like meeting all of Gary's friends, I remembered I had the perfect thing. On our honeymoon, one of our stops was in Las Vegas. We were doing a little shopping and I fell in love with a quite unusual ensemble. It was silver silk pants with a matching sleeveless jacket decorated with beautiful and ornate embroidery throughout.

It was certainly not something you would ever see in Czech Republic and probably not Texas either. I had never worn anything like it before in my life, but it was so beautiful and for some reason, it made me feel very elegant and tall. So, when we were deciding about my wedding attire for the party, I did not picture myself in any kind of wedding gown, especially since it was a really late wedding reception. I decided to wear the silver silk outfit we purchased in Las Vegas.

After I had selected my attire, one of my friends asked me if I was going to have my hair and makeup done for the reception. Honestly, I never even thought about it. I never had my makeup or hair done before. So, I decided, why not? I asked a couple people for beautician recommendations and made an appointment for the afternoon of the party. The day of the party arrived and just hours before guests were to arrive, I was sitting in the stylist's chair. Since I didn't have any particular style in mind, they asked me what I was wearing. I passionately described this beautiful Asian silk sleeveless jacket with beautiful silver embroidery and then let them have creative liberty. And creative liberty they had!

Back home, Gary was working on final details for the party. He is very hands on and creative when it comes to decorating and catering, so we took care of a large part of the reception ourselves. When I walked in the door from my appointment, just before the party was scheduled to begin, Gary could hardly recognize me. He turned around with a puzzled look on his face, not knowing who this woman was standing in front of him! My hair was swept up in a twist, and my make-up was almost theatrical with a sophisticated Asian flare—very different from the simple country girl he just married! The beauticians did a great job matching my hair and makeup to the attire I described, however, it didn't match me! To be honest, I could hardly recognize myself in the mirror! Gary just looked at me and smiled, as he often does. There certainly wasn't any time to worry about it or do anything about it by then. Guests would be arriving any moment, so I hurried to get dressed and get back out to greet our company. I took a deep breath, not feeling quite like myself. We both stood at the door and as I was receiving guests, I was feeling quite self-conscious. I could only imagine what Gary's friends were thinking of this woman he just up and married! Of course, I introduced myself and graciously thanked them for coming to celebrate with us, but I also was very quick to let people know that I don't normally look like this!

We had a great time that night and everyone enjoyed the wonderful food, drinks and music. To be honest,

I don't think people really cared that I did not look myself and really, as the night went on, I didn't care either. At the end of the party, after the last guest went home, I went in the bathroom feeling like Cinderella as I pulled about 60 bobby pins and clipped flowers out of my hair.

Even though it was technically our wedding celebration, there are no photos from that evening displayed anywhere in our home because no one would recognize me! I do have them saved in the album though. The pictures I do have displayed in our home, are from our vow renewal service, that took place five years later with my family in Czech Republic. Since my parents were unable to attend our wedding or our wedding reception, we decided to celebrate yet again with them. It was also my dad's 50th birthday, and we had a lot of family gathering together already to celebrate him. I coordinated with my cousin and my mom and sister and we surprised my dad.

Our vow renewal in the Czech Republic was in the fall of 2004. This was almost five years after my parents first met Gary. The first time they met him was in February 2000. February is also ball season in my country—gown not sports. Each town would have a formal ball or a masquerade ball. That year, our town was having a masquerade ball. Remember, in my small town in the mountains, everyone knows everyone, and our arrival was much anticipated. I don't believe my hometown was ever visited by an American before, so it was event for sure. For most people in my town, what they knew about America is what they saw on TV and what they knew about Texas was from watching the show "Dallas." So, Gary's nickname quickly became "J.R." or at least my grandma called him that. She loved that series! We all did. When we arrived at the masquerade ball, Gary very cleverly flipped his long hair which he had at that time, over his face and put sunglasses over it and we walked in. Gary was Cousin It from the Munster's TV show. People didn't know what to think! Finally, after about 20 minutes or so, Gary took his mask off and presented himself as my husband--the Texas guy! We had a great time with my family and friends. Of course, no one spoke any English, so I was translating all the conversations with my very broken English.

By the time we went back in 2004 for my dad's birthday, they all knew and loved Gary. It was the perfect time to have our surprise wedding vow renewal. I bought a simple wedding dress and Gary brought a tuxedo with him from Texas. We coordinated with the musicians to play a wedding song, and before our surprise ceremony, Gary walked over to my dad and asked for my hand in marriage. (Better late than never.) Of course he agreed. The wedding music played, we renewed our vows, and my dad and I were able to finally have our first dance.

The following day I coordinated with one of our local photographers, whom I had known since I was a little girl, to take pictures of Gary and I in our wedding attire in one of the local nature parks. In those pictures my make up is minimal like I normally wear it and I cherish those photos and the memory.

It's funny how make up, or lack thereof can seem to be so "defining" for a woman. I rarely wear makeup, I guess because I do not want to deal with removing it, or even thinking about it, or needing fussing to pack it for my trips and such. Gary says he doesn't care for me to wear makeup anyway, so I'm generally not wearing it unless there is a special occasion.

My story with makeup started when I was in 7th grade or so. We had an outdoor school event with activities for children, music, and different vendors. It was pretty much the celebration of this end of the school year. My mom was helping, volunteering at one of the booths, and I decided to put makeup on before I went to the event. When I arrived, as soon as my Mom saw me and she realized I put makeup on, she sent me right back home to remove it. I was feeling so embarrassed, and ashamed. And as a good girl who was taught to always be compliant, I did what I was told and went home to remove the makeup. For me, this was a pivotal moment that impacted my perception of myself wearing makeup. Looking back, I know I was too young, but it was pretty dramatic for a young teen girl and affected me the rest of my life.

Years later, when I was discussing this with my mom, she shared a story with me. One time, in her early 20's she had her hair and makeup done for an event, and it did not look at all like her. She was so embarrassed to go in public looking like that, she went and closed herself in the restroom, and removed her makeup, and straightened her hair. To this day you would rarely see my mom with makeup on, and really almost never; so I guess I come by it honestly.

After the whirlwind of our wedding and honeymoon, I knew I needed to start thinking about the next chapter of my career. Everything I had planned up until that point was off the table because I was living permanently in America. Because I had a dual degree from Czech Republic as a pediatric nurse and in physical therapy, naturally, I thought I would be able to start working in one of my respective fields in the U.S. right away. However, I soon learned, after numerous rejection letters, that my education did not transfer so I couldn't get a license to do either in the U.S. This was extremely disheartening. It was everything I had been working for my entire life and in order for me to work in either one of the fields, I would need to start all over again. On top of that, I didn't pass the TOE-FL test, which is the Test of English as a Foreign Language. I didn't learn English "by the book" I learned by subtitles and speaking with people. I didn't grasp the grammar rules and I was feeling very discouraged about my future in America.

One day, Gary received a call from a friend of a friend. This couple had just came home from the hospital with their newborn and felt completely overwhelmed and asked if I could help them. They wanted me to be their baby nurse. I was so excited. I drove to their home as soon as I could, ready to help these new parents on their journey of parenthood. I spent a couple of weeks with them, primarily at night, until they felt more comfortable, and helped them understand their baby boy's needs.

That phone call started a whole new chapter in my life. I became known as the Baby Nurse for Houston families. One connection led to another and then another and I loved every bit of it. I loved what I was doing, and I was able to incorporate my knowledge and my passion to help others care for their babies. That was over 20 year ago when I formed my first company called "Loving Infant Care." I began training other women on my methods of helping new families and eventually, formed my next business which is now the "Motherhood Center." This allowed me to incorporate even more offerings and allowed me to draw on my physical therapy background with introduction of prenatal exercises, massage and of course developing various educational programs and curriculum.

The internet was brand new and there certainly weren't many websites or resources at that time. I had to rely on my instincts, intuition, and personal experience to develop the resources we needed. Truthfully, I didn't want to be influenced by anyone, or give over any control of the business, so even if there were opportunities for partnerships or joint ventures, I stayed singularly focused. Perhaps it was the way I was raised in Communism and the history of my family with the beliefs that you really can't trust anyone.

One time, I was asked a question in regards to mentorship, and if I had many mentors throughout my career, and honestly with a little bit of embarrassment I shared that I have not. I was starting to really think about my answer, and what the reasons might be for not seeking out mentors. Although I did have plenty of business women in my networking groups, I have never sought out personal mentors. As I've been processing some of my experiences from the past, I realized that for me, the sensitivity of the information I'm giving and what influences I had in the past, what information to trust, I had gotten to the point that I was primarily relying on my own thoughts, my own experiences to make decisions. I was afraid to be influenced by others and possibly their agendas. I know it sounds silly but that was and is my reality. So without having any mentors in the field, I pioneered the industry over 20 years ago.

So often when you work in your business, it's hard to see the successes and accomplishments until you receive some recognition or validation. Of course, we receive many compliments and testimonials from our clients, almost on a daily basis, but I feel like my biggest recognition of the impact of the business is when there is a press story written about it, or when I get invited to share expert opinions for different TV stations here in Houston. This happened several times a year and I love to share about the business, on air or in the TV studio. I enjoy sharing my knowledge and accomplishments of the Motherhood Center. Just recently, due to the pandemic, I did a few interviews through Zoom, and its amazing how we can adapt. Because of the unique concept I created, our business has been fortunate enough to gain exposure through many media and newspaper outlets over the years.

My goal, and something I share with all of my team, is to strive for 100% client satisfaction. I know it's not always possible, but it's most definitely our goal. Honestly if we cannot for some reason deliver 100% satisfaction, or if we have an unhappy client, it sincerely hurts me. I feel such a defeat and sadness because I want every client not only to be happy, but to be extremely happy! These moms, dads, and their babies deserve that.

I do have to say that after 20 years in business and over 35,000 clients, we were able to make the vast majority of our clients extremely happy. I'm pleased with that and proud of that, but also never want to let go of the 100% satisfaction desire. We are always trying to find ways to improve, innovate, create new business opportunities and new offerings and services for our clients.

We are in the caretaking and caregiving business, but also being the sage advisor and educator for our families. Many of our educators, instructors, massage therapists and caregivers have been with me for over ten years. My team and staff are truly an extension of my family. Especially since my family is not here, besides my husband's family which I of course adore, now I feel like I have thousands of extended family members here in America. I feel very fortunate and lucky!

Over the years, and various challenges and hardships, constantly thinking, marketing, changing, updating, failing and getting up and starting again, I learned that every mistake is an opportunity to learn, change, redirect and grow. I read somewhere recently that when you fail and start over, you are not starting from zero, you are starting from experience.

There have been many tempting partnerships over the years with different businesses, corporations, and when I looked further into those, I learned that I would have to change concepts, or change who I am, our mission and vision is, oftentimes I have decided to pass on those opportunities. For me honesty and integrity is all that I have. I would never want to sell out my clients or do something just because it would be a good deal for me. I always have clients' well-being in mind first. I truly run my business from my heart, always trying to make sure that I surround myself with like-minded people, with passion and desire to care and help others.

As I mentioned before, over the years there have been numerous articles and write-ups about the Motherhood Center and myself. I always make sure to send a copy of those articles to my parents, although they don't read in English, they always like to receive it and carefully store it. It really is just for them to enjoy, as they are not people who like to show off, and they don't want look like they are bragging.

Often I send them video clips from the TV coverages I've been on, but of course they don't understand those either, but I guess it's not bad for this girl from small mountain village to be on the front cover of prominent Business Journal or being recognized by the Senator for the work she has done for moms and children in Houston. But that success didn't happen overnight.

Early on when I started out, my understanding of business practices was limited. I did not have a business background, so I lacked confidence in that area. But I just kept pushing forward, learning and growing along the way. I trusted my instincts and I trusted that I knew what my clients needed. When I began marketing though, I wasn't sure what to do so I started reaching out to obstetricians. When I first started setting up meetings or visiting doctor's offices, the only example I had of how to market to a doctor's office was the drug reps I saw going in and out. So, I did what I saw them do. I would dress in a dark pant suit, starched shirt, jacket and heals, and even had a roller cart with my materials. Over the years, my confidence got stronger and my attire became a little more relaxed as I shifted my focus to relate more to the mothers. Nowadays, I feel pretty comfortable in jeans and a white starched shirt...but I still wear my high heels, of course!

Wanting to build my credibility, I thought often about getting my MBA or taking some business courses or accounting classes. However, I already had a business to run which was more than a full time job! I really couldn't take on a college program with that so instead, in my spare time, I would read business articles or business books, and learn all I could on my own. I have always enjoyed learning, so anything related to business has always been of interest to me. I would also sign myself up for different networking events, pushing myself out of my comfort zone on a weekly, if not daily, basis. Even if I did not know anyone at those events, I knew I could meet people and network. In a way, it was nice to be there by myself, because I could really just focus on what I needed from the event or leave at whatever point I needed to in order to get back to work or home.

One of the reasons I was so focused on immersing myself into the American culture and growing my business was because, in a way, it was self-preservation. It hurt too much to think about what I left behind in my home country. The fact that I came to America in my early twenties, in the middle of so much change in the Czech Republic, from politics to the economy, to people's relationships; it was hard to live in two worlds. It was painful to think of my family during that time when I couldn't communicate with them as much as I wanted to. I just had to shift my focus to my life in America.

The fact that I was able to go see my family once a year was huge. I often reflect on the people who left for America while escaping communism knowing that they might not ever see their family again. I was grateful that I had the opportunity to go back and see them.

One of my first trips going back home to Czech Republic. I didn't realize how "Americanized" I had become. I had been living in a major U.S. city with a population of almost six million people which was half the population of my home country! I was back in Czech Republic only a day and was headed for dinner with some friends. We were walking through town and I just had a whole new appreciation for all the historical buildings and ornate architecture, so different from city life in Houston. I had the urge to stop and stare at these buildings that had been around since the 1700's or older! I was just taking in their beauty and the stories they could share. As we still had ten more minutes to walk, my friends ask me what was going on and why

I was pausing so much. I shared with them, how precious it is to see such history and so much culture in these buildings, and how much they should appreciate these buildings and what they have to offer. Of course, they just laughed and didn't take me very seriously, but who knows, maybe one day they will realize it as well. Sometimes we have to take a step back to really appreciate what we have.

On another trip back home a couple of years later, I had a little different experience. A group of us were again walking to a restaurant, and I found myself way ahead of everyone. Rather than enjoying my friends and the sites around me, I was so focused on getting to where we were going that I was walking faster than anyone else. They actually had to yell at me because I had gotten so far ahead! "Where are you running off to?" I realized I was just "on a mission" again coming from the big city where you are always in motion, always on a mission, just going, going, going! And that's when I realized—and even more so after spending two or three weeks in the Czech Republic—how different my two lifestyles are. In Czech Republic, people spend a lot of time in the forest, in nature, surrounded by a pretty simplistic way of living. When I would return to Houston, I would try to hold on to that sense of peacefulness and simplicity for as long as I could. I have to say that usually within a week, I was completely immersed back into the big city way of life. I have to put much intention and effort into preserving the simplicity of life and seeking opportunities to just be still and quiet. I'm very intentional to find balance between the two worlds I love—the city life with all the opportunities it provides, but also enjoying nature, small towns, and the countryside, which allows me to recharge and reconnect with myself.

My regular travels with Gary help a lot as well, and we have created so many wonderful memories together. Some are short trips to our friend's ranches, or their vacation homes, or sometimes longer trips across the states.

CHAPTER EIGHT

Yeehaw to New Adventures

I was married for a few years when my mom and dad finally agreed to come to see us in Houston. Not that they did not want it to come earlier, but not knowing English and pretty much having never left our home village, except for a couple of short vacation trips to nearby towns, this was pretty much the biggest adventure for them in their entire lives. It was their first flight ever and somehow without any knowledge of the English language, they managed to get to Houston, although I'm certain it was a quite dramatic and overwhelming for both of them. My parents are both reserved in new situations. They are small town "homebodies" who are frugal and like their routines. They don't like to obligate other people either.

We picked them up at the airport and brought them straight to my American home. It was wonderful to have them here and I was eager to show them around.

I couldn't wait show them my business, my friends, my favorite restaurants, shops and of course, our airplane.

We didn't have any specific trips planned, we usually don't. We prefer to be spontaneous, and seize whatever opportunities present themselves and decide from there. So, on the third morning of their visit to America, as we were finishing up breakfast, I felt like it was time to leave town. They would be here for three weeks, but I thought it would be nice to have lunch in Santa Fe, New Mexico. I pitched the idea to Gary, and since he is as spontaneous as me, he said, "Sure! Why not?" So, we got ready and packed an overnight travel bag, just in case we wanted to stay the night. This was my parent's first private plane ride, and my mom was definitely very nervous. My dad on the other hand, was smiling, and feeling a little giddy on the inside.

I knew that they would enjoy seeing Santa Fe. Growing up, we had primarily only Czech movies, and few movies recorded in other Soviet countries, rarely we had movies from Western Europe, or America, and all of them were dubbed, so it really felt like they were Czech-made movies. (Czech people are known for great dubbing.) One of the movies I remember from childhood, was a German movie series about handsome Apache chief's son Winnetou and German engineer Old Shatterhand. The two of them destined to be blood brothers to prevent all-out war. These movie series were filmed in beautiful nature settings, with big rivers, canyons and mountains.

The movie was the closest experience to the Indian culture that we could have imagined. When we arrived in Santa Fe, my parents took in the rich, Indian culture with charming adobe homes, colorful clothing, jewelry and pottery. My parents were loving it and we decided to stay a couple of extra nights to explore Santa Fe and the area and the surroundings more.

As we were taking off in the airplane and headed back to Houston, my husband realized that we are fairly close to the Grand Canyon and that would be a great opportunity for my parents to see this spectacular wonder of the world, so we decided to change our heading, and fly that direction. At that point, neither one of my parents could hold back the excitement! As we were flying and viewing the rock spires along the way, then the rim of the canyon, before landing at the airport. Seeing the Grand Canyon for the first time is awe-inspiring. The awesomeness of the Grand Canyon is so hard to capture with a camera. You can't fully grasp the vastness, the mystery, the colors.

We decided to have lunch at the famous lodge, Bright Angel, before heading back to Houston. While we were in a taxi heading back to the airport our driver asked if we were visiting from Las Vegas. We told him that we are not, and that we are actually from Houston, just showing my parents around. Of course, that conversation sparked a little idea for my husband since he enjoys showing people a good time. As I mentioned before, my parents don't like to inconvenience anyone, even if means they don't get to experience something or have to miss out. But Gary trained my mother to stop saying "nei, nie, nie" which means "no, no, no" to start saying, "Yeehaw to new adventures!" But even still, we decided not to tell them this new idea that Gary had until we were landing in Las Vegas. Gary arranged to have a limo pick us all up at the airport and take us to our hotel. This was more than my parents could have ever imagined happening to them their entire lives. I knew how they might be feeling as I thought about my travels to the South of France years prior.

As soon as we arrived at our hotel and checked into our suite, again such a new experience for my parents, we encouraged them to just relax, maybe lay down for a little bit in the king size bed or take a jacuzzi bath. My parents of course could not do either. Instead, they pulled up their chairs to the floor-to-ceiling windows and could not stop looking outside at all the lights, buildings, flashing signs and activities of the Las Vegas life.

While we were all settling in, we received a phone call from one of our dear friends and learned that a group was coming to Las Vegas for Wildcatters annual convention. Of course, at that point, we realized that our overnight bag with just a few pieces of clothing would not be enough to really explore Las Vegas. After we learned that our friends invited us to join them in some of the activities and convention parties, Gary and I had to go shopping. We had to go buy pretty much everything new. From a belt to socks, to my dress and pretty much everything we needed from head to toe. My parents were quite overwhelmed and of course never even dreamed of visiting Las Vegas, something they just saw in the movies. They were not too comfortable to join us for these activities, and with zero English, I had already been translating everything. They wouldn't have enjoyed themselves so they decided that they would prefer to stay in the hotel and explore activities there. We showed them where to get a meal, which was a whole new experience as well, as my parents never experienced a Vegas-style buffet. My dad had to learn not to overfill his plate at the first station, because there were many more stations to try. Needless to say, my parents are still talking about those buffet stations in Las Vegas.

After spending a couple more days in Las Vegas it was time for us to head back to H-Town. As we were flying back through West Texas, it was getting close to sunset, and my dad shared through the headsets, that it looks just like in the Marlboro commercials— the mountain structures, open lands, the color of the mountains during the sunset. And with that, we quickly decided to land in West Texas, so my parents could truly experience the feel, and see the look of that part of the state. After landing, we went to a local steak restaurant in a Texas style setting. Just another wonderful experience for my parents to store in their memories. The next day we decided it was time for us to go back to Houston for real.

After spending a couple days in Houston, we decided to show my parents my "third" home, my first home being of course the Czech Republic, Houston being my second, and Port Aransas Mustang Island being the third. I knew my parents would love being there, seeing the ocean for the first time. I knew this was going to be a great experience for them and of course it was. We rented a house close to the beach with a swimming pool and my parents spent much time on the beach, collecting seashells, and sunbathing. They made a goal to go back home with a suntan since there was still snow on the ground in Czech Republic. We had a great time, taking them on boat rides and exploring local restaurants and cooking. When it was time to head back to Houston after a few days, we were midway back to Houston and decided to have one more stop. One of our dear friend's family owns an island which is basically a long strip of large fluffy beaches with an airstrip. As soon as we landed, my parents headed straight to the beach, which was mostly untouched. My parents started exploring and picking up all the new shells. They were giddy and as excited as kids in Candy Land. We had just a couple hours to stop there before we headed back to Houston. My parents traded their shell collection for even bigger ones.

I was so glad that I was able to show my parents around on their first trip to America, and let them see some of my favorite places, as well as exploring places with them. It was great to have my parents in my home, and eat breakfast, lunch and dinner with them, and really let them be a part of my life in America. Naturally, it was hard to say goodbye when it was time for them to go back home. I was very nervous for them and they were as well about the flight back home. Now they had to deal with the overwhelm of the airports and the language barrier on their own. Perhaps I was more nervous about the reality that they would probably never come back to America. But I savored every moment with them, as we all should with the people we love.

CHAPTER NINE

Czeching Out

Growing up, I didn't have many dreams or desires. I was a pretty content and happy child. I liked hiking and being outdoors, but I was never the one looking up in the skies and dreaming about flying to the moon, or really flying anywhere at all. As I mentioned earlier, my first flight ever was flying across the "big pond" to America and then just a few months later, I became a huge fan of flying—all thanks to Bonanza 57GG, our six-seater plane.

I love the spontaneity flying offers. Flying brings me such a sense of freedom. It allows me to completely check out from everything else going on in the world. In the air, you can't make phone calls, check emails, or send text messages. You are forced to be in the moment. I had only been in the United States around four months when I had that first trip in Gary's private plane to King Ranch in South Texas. After that, we traveled almost every weekend, or at least every other weekend. I have so many great memories flying around America. The truth is it's like a time machine, as my husband calls it, and I think he's right. Time seems to stand still when we are in the air and I love every moment of it. The first time I heard Gary talking on the radio I fell in love! I fell in love with him, with the voice on the radio, and I fell in love with the whole experience. Since then, I've flown in the co-pilot seat for almost two thousand hours and counting!

As the "co-pilot," my primary focus and responsibilities are to watch the instruments, keep my pilot company, and just be. When we have longer flights, I prepare a snack or lunch, and play flight attendant. I love those long flights, when I have the opportunity to see all the different landscapes and topographies throughout America. I love flying to places like the Bahamas and seeing hundreds of little islands and crystal clear blue waters. I also love landing on an island airstrip and being picked up at the plane by locals in a golf cart, to our island resort. I equally love flying over the Rocky Mountains, where it feels like you can reach out the window and touch the mountain peaks covered in snow, or flying along the coast of California and seeing whales splashing their tails in the great ocean, or watching the waves crash on the rocky shores, or flying over desert lands where it can take hours before you see your neighbor. Flying over the Arizona mountains is completely breathtaking! The landscape is so full of colors and incredible sunsets. Over the Nevada desert, the colors on the ground seem almost fluorescent. It's amazing how you can see all the different seasons from the air. You can see the leaves changing on aspen trees in Colorado, the amazing West Texas land in mountain structures. Then there are the vast lakes in Michigan or landing at night in Las Vegas, the city which never sleeps. We have flown through sunrises to sunsets, storms and lighting, and through beautiful fireworks that light up the night skies. Every trip is so special and gives us the opportunity to really see how great the country really is and how much it has to offer.

When you are the pilot's wife, your role is a little different than just being a passenger. There are many factors to consider before flying, most importantly the weather. Gary has been flying over 50 years now, and we always consider the weather and adjust our flight plans accordingly. We never take chances regarding the weather, but there are certainly times when the weather patterns evolve while we were in the air. One of the many things I like about flying it forces you to be living in the moment. There is no time to think about silly things or get lost in the future planning. There are many instruments to watch, other airplanes flying around, you have to listen to the radio, watch for the birds when you are taking off or landing. Even though you may be fully prepared and focused, you are still operating a mechanical machine, ten thousand feet up in the air. Anything can go wrong.

On one of the flights we had, flying to Colorado via New Mexico, we learned that the President was is the air, which means all aircraft and all radio and traffic control people are on a high alert. Soon after we were notified, our radios went out for no apparent reason. The fact that not only the primary radio but also the backup radio was not functioning became very concerning. We were at about eight thousand feet elevation, not able to communicate, and of course not knowing the exact pattern of the presidential flight, or if we were in the path, so we had to take the plane down as soon as possible for security reasons. Since we were not able to let other aircrafts know where we were or any nearby airports know that we were preparing to land, we had to quickly locate a small airport, assuming that there would be very little traffic to be able to land safely. And we did. The airport manager was a little surprised when we showed up unannounced, but we explained the situation. Thankfully, there was a radio shop on the property which allowed us to get a loaner radio so we could continue on our journey.

Another time, we were flying to South Texas when all electronics on the plane went down. Everything. Again, with no communication with ground control or radio, or other planes, we knew we needed to bring the airplane down as soon as possible. In this situation, I had to say, I lost my cool a bit and this was way more serious than the last time. My emotions were high, and I could not even think for a moment. Then my pilot husband asked me to climb to the back seat and wait for his prompt to manually bring the wheels down. Yes, since none of the electronics worked, the whole plane needed to be operated manually. If you have ever done that before, you might know, although it is a simple mechanic, it requires you to turn a metal handle in a certain direction, about 50 times. I started to raise my voice, I started to get uncomfortable, the plane felt like it became louder. While flying 200 miles an hour I had to remove my headset and climb to the back of the plane and physically bring the wheels of the airplane down. I began to crank the handle over and over again. After a few minutes, my husband asked me if I did what I needed to do, and if the wheels where all the way down. I didn't know how to answer that. There was no way for me to know! I had never done this before, and I certainly couldn't go outside and look. I had to trust myself that I did all I could. I climbed back to into my co-pilot seat and said a little prayer as the ground came closer and closer. I believe I said one more little prayer right before the wheels hit the ground, and thankfully they did. I was never more grateful to be on the ground than I was that day.

A few summers ago, we were flying out of the Texas Hill Country. We had a wonderful trip, we always do. Those hilly peaks remind me so much of my homeland, and it's one of the closest areas which feels mountain-ous, and still close to Houston. We took off, and then a couple minutes into the flight, my door opened! Yes, in the air, flying about a hundred fifty miles an hour my airplane door flew open. I could not be prepared for this experience! I was trying to somehow hold on to that door which of course I was not really able to do, but that was my instinct and the only thing I could think of at that moment. My pilot calmly turned the airplane around and we prepared for landing, letting the airport tower know that "I forgot something." I can assure you, from then on, I double and triple check that the door is securely latched every single time. But my instinct is still to hold on to the door at takeoff. As I mentioned before, you always need to be in the present moment when flying, always stay aware.

Even though we love flying, we often took weekend road trips around Texas as well. One of my first trips outside of Houston, was to the nearby city of Austin about two and a half hours away. We were driving on I-10 heading west when all of the sudden I started to see country roads that had the names of villages near to my hometown in Czech Republic. I was in complete shock and disbelief and could not understand why. Soon after, one of my friends gave me a book about Czech pioneers in Texas. Because of my broken English, I could not fully read it initially, and honestly I was a little confused about the word "pioneers" because during communism, I was a pioneer, which meant something totally different. Now I understand. It's fascinating to read about the early settlers, and where the Czech pioneers settled in the Texas hills along the Colorado River between Columbus and La Grange. The topography is similar to Czech Republic so I can see the draw for the Czech settlers, along with Polish and Germans.

Reading that book made me see the incredible bravery, the emotions they had, leaving their families behind, and getting on a boat with just a little to their name, and finding a land to call their home. It really truly resonates with me. I cannot even imagine, starting from scratch like that. At least I had a suitcase! I'm proud of my pioneering heritage. I'm proud that I pioneered in business, and I'm proud that I came to America like the brave men and women before me. I guess you can say that the word pioneer has a lot of meanings for me.

One of our most memorable road trips was a 17-day trip with "Mr. Green Jeans." One of my clients who hired one of our baby nurses to care of her twins for three months, lived in Jackson Hole, Wyoming. She invited us to come spend a few days with her at her ranch. We flew from Houston to Canyon City, Colorado where we had our 1978 Ford camping truck waiting for us, affectionately known as Mr. Green Jeans. We stored it in Colorado for mountain exploring trips. Our first stop was at the grocery store to stock up on all kinds of goodies, before we hit the road up in the mountains. It would take several days before we reached my client's house, but we planned to camp in the national parks on our way there, we would hike the canyons, explore old dinosaur sites, and enjoy the beauty of nature. I love camping, I grew up camping and hiking, but we used to call it "tramping." Yes tramping, I know it's not a word you would normally use, much less call yourself a tramp! But in Europe it was a movement that started back in the 1920's, where people would go hiking and enjoy nature, oftentimes not having a certain destination in mind. The goal was simply to be in nature with friends, playing guitars, relaxing and possibly having a beer or two. Oftentimes the songs we sang were anti-communism, about democracy, and our desire for freedom. Although tramping was not illegal, it was not supported by the communist regime either. But we still did it and I have so many great memories. I loved to be able to breathe the fresh air and listen to the birds. I even love the physical exhaustion of carrying a heavy backpack and when you still have few miles ahead, just pushing myself, and my mind to persevere. In the end there's a great reward of a campfire meal where canned goods taste amazing because everything tastes so much better after a long day of physical exertion! On our tramping trips, we would bathe in the rivers, or sneak into a restaurant bathroom along the trails, and quickly wash our hair in the sink. I always had short hair since I can remember so it was a very quick wash without anyone even knowing. And then there were times we would get rained on and wake up in a soaking wet sleeping bag, but we definitely learned lessons from that, like how important it is to set up your tent properly and where to set it up. Early in our relationship, Gary and I had numerous camping trips where we took our four-wheel drive

Ford pickup truck, loaded it with camping gear, and found unique camping sites. I learned that camping with Gary can be a quite different from what I experienced in my childhood. Our Ford pickup truck would be loaded with all kinds of goodies for camping. From the very large tent, sleeping bags to queen-size air mattress, kitchen gear, fake green grass carpet to set up in the "kitchen" area. We would have a cooler filled with steaks, all kinds of great salami, fresh veggies, and so much more.

So back to our 17-day trip...there we were driving through the Colorado mountains in our "Mr. Green Jeans" old four-wheel drive truck which allowed us to really explore some very unique places that other cars could not go. We selected a destination camp site by a "pristine" creek. We were about two hours away when we encountered a fairly good-sized tree laying perfectly across our tiny little road. Because of the thickness of the forest, there was no way to go around it. If we would have turned around, it would have been several hours back to a place we could camp for the night but yet we were two hours from our destination, so, we decided to tackle the tree. Thankfully, Gary had an ax and a saw in the back of the truck bed for just such an occasion. We knew this was going to be a good amount of work, so we took turns chopping this tree. We spent an hour chopping and sawing this tree. Finally, what a great reward it was when we were able to get the trunk separated and then tie one end to the trunk and drag it out of the way of the road. Mr. Green Jeans came through again! It was a very empowering experience. Dinner that night at camp tasted especially incredible.

When we finally arrived at my client's home, she was a very gracious host and we spent a few days at her mountain guest house. We explored the area a little more before heading back. As we were getting close to town with our airplane, Gary had an idea of maybe getting a little "civilized and cleaned up" before heading back to Houston. We decided to have one more stop, which was at the Hotel Broadmoor in Colorado Springs. The Broadmoor is a beautiful luxury resort built in 1918. As we were pulling up in our very dusty green camping truck, we were definitely getting looks, as it was not the usual vehicle arriving at the luxurious hotel. We got out and asked the valet to wait for us since we didn't know if we would have a room. We walked up to the reception desk and Gary shared a story about how his parents celebrated their honeymoon there. I wasn't sure if the story happened the way he told it but the lady felt compelled to give us the honeymoon suite. Once we had our key and room number, we went to the bellman to get our suitcases/backpacks from the truck bed. The bellman climbed into the rugged truck to get our belongings and then dusted off his crisp black suit jacket. By the time we got to our room, the champagne and beautiful flowers were awaiting us! It was wonderful and I was so ready to take a bath. As I was drawing the bath water, the view from our window was right down the entrance of the hotel. To my disbelief, our dusty old green truck was still there 30 min later! I thought for sure they would have removed it immediately, but I guess they found it entertaining to have it there . We got cleaned up and had a nice dinner and the next day we fly back home. Gary and I still laugh about the experience.

CHAPTER TEN

Defining Moments

Gary was a member of the local Country club which I joined when we got married. I started to play golf and really enjoyed it, although the majority of the ladies who played golf were around 30 years older than me. My friends who were my age were mostly mothers of young kids, so they didn't have time to play golf. Being an entrepreneur and business owner, I was able to carve out a little me time and enjoy the club.

One fall morning, I was in the locker room with a group of ladies getting ready to play golf. The news was on the TV as we were talking, and a breaking report came in. It was the most unimaginable event happening right in front of our eyes. It was September 11th and we stood there and watched the twin towers get hit by airplanes in New York City. We were shocked but still heading out to the golf course as we intended. After about 30 minutes, we just couldn't continue. We couldn't focus on anything else, so we returned back to the locker room, and went to our homes, scared, overwhelmed, and confused. Thinking about it now, it feels just like yesterday. A patriotic spirit rose up in me, and in the people of America—the camaraderie, the connection we experienced was beautiful and overwhelming. My love and commitment to this country became deeply ingrained in me, and the sense of freedom which I experienced after communism fell, quickly was challenged. Just as I was starting to understand democracy and truly appreciate freedom, what happened on 9/11 shook me to the core. Thousands of innocent lives lost and families across the country devastated and broken. And at the same time, an incredible outpouring of solidarity and care came from around the world. Thousands of volunteers, fire fighters, police, military, healthcare workers, and people coming out of retirement to help fellow Americans. We were all scared, and confused, puzzled about how this would affect us individually, our businesses, our families, and our country over the long term. That event had a tremendous and lasting impact on me and the way I approach my service to others. I have always been empathetic and compassionate, and after 9/11 just a little bit more so.

During the season I was building my business and

developing my brand, often there were times where I felt a little bit overwhelmed and lost in the emotions that come with being an entrepreneur and also when caring for others. When the phone rings, you truly never know who will be on the other end of the line needing help or what kind of help they may need. For about the first 12 years or so of the business, I was on call seven days a week, taking calls at 7:00 in the morning or at 10:00 at night no matter if it was Saturday, Sunday or a holiday. On top of that, throughout the years, there have been times that I had to borrow money from family or friends, take out business loans, having all of my credit cards maxed out completely, having many employees and contractors depending on me, and on the success of the business. I was under such pressure that I had to step back and embrace the truth that the success of my business, or possible failure, does not define me. It's easy to mix up our "who" with our "do."

I would often think about what I would do if I did not have my business, or what I would do if the business would fail. I would think of the skills I have, the experiences I had from growing my business, or what I could apply in other fields. There would be times that I would think about having another job to support my current business. Some strange and very different jobs and positions come to my mind. A gardener, I love trimming trees, flowers, and plants. Oftentimes when I have a hard day, or I'm frustrated or need to express some energy, I would get my gardening gloves on, and clippers and head to our backyard, start trimming plants, bushes, start clipping vines, making flower arrangements, trimming palm trees and find myself being expressive and creative. Sometimes my husband needs to stop me, as I can get pretty vagarious with the clippers and maybe give the shrubs a little bit too much of a haircut. But I love to see things evolve and grow, and to be able to nurture and reap the benefits of our garden.

The other job which would be a little bit more natural to my experience would be becoming a Governess or Butler. My nature is to take care of others, make others feel better, more comfortable, and help take care of things which makes life easier for others. Another thought I often have is starting Bed and Breakfast creating comfort and great recommendations for my guests. Fortunately, because of hard work and perseverance, I'm able to continue to grow my business but knowing that my business does not define me is very important. Having a realization like that enables me to grow my business with a more open perspective. And there were times when making a career change, seemed like an easier route. Especially when a legal issue would arise. Not that it happened often, but once is really enough. Any type of court battle takes a toll on you emotionally. It feels like going through divorce or a bad custody battle. I've had several legal battles and even when I was in the right, the stress of it all and the money I spent on legal fees was overwhelming. I remember being so upset, confused and feeling defeated, because even though I wanted to take the high road, or wanted to believe that truth will prevail, when you're in a situation like this, it really seems it boils down to how good or well-connected your attorney is or his relationship with the judge! And so often it's not about whether you are right or wrong.

Those times were so hard emotionally, and I had to remain very strong—strong for my company, strong for myself, my family. I had to create balance and keep focusing on the growth of the business, while trying to find meaning in all of it. Of course, years later I realized that because of the experiences I had, I'm better prepared for the future, and able to address things differently or know what to look for if I should be in a similar situation again, but hopefully avoid it all together.

When people gain power, it changes their personalities, and they want more, despite hurting someone else in the process. You might have a friend who you thought was completely supportive, and they can turn around and stab you in the back, and then they find some reason to justify it in the end.

One time, I was so upset I needed to have someone help me process the experience and find a way to get beyond this anger, frustration, and hurt feelings. I spoke to psychologist who has worked with a lot of business owners and she helped me see the big picture a little bit better. She shared with me that by giving this person all of my emotional energy it is like holding one end of an imaginary rope and creating energy for the other person to pull back. I needed to stop the tug of war and reframe my thoughts by changing what I focused on. This gave me the power to find a place of calmness within me that I could go back to whenever I needed. And of course, I was not necessarily giving up on the battle, but I needed to find other ways to fight, not just in my mind which was only hurting myself and draining my emotional energy.

I have to say, it was not easy. Now, years later strangely, I'm grateful for that experience. On one of the days when I felt like I was at my lowest point, with no energy to deal with all the mess, I received a call from one of my trusted friends. She shared with me in such a powerful way that I still remember her guidance and advice all these years later. But what I didn't know, and learned several months later after our call, is that my friend was going through a very difficult situation herself. Despite her own hardship, she was there for me on the phone, supporting and guiding me, and lending a listening ear. Honestly, compared to what she was going through, my "big problem" was nothing. Later on, I was able to be there for her as someone she could lean on and trust when she needed me.

You truly never know what someone else may be going through. Too often, we are too quick to judge others not knowing the full story. So, the next time you find yourself in a situation where you feel like you are unable to handle it, or that it's bigger than you, find some grounding points. Tell yourself, "I know this is going to pass." One day, you will be able to look back and see how you have grown from that experience.

One of the lawsuits I was party to was close to trial and depositions were scheduled. This legal issue was about a verbal business agreement I had with someone. I knew I was in the right and I was ready to fight for my company which was like my baby. Having never been in a deposition before, I didn't know what to expect. I just knew there would be an opposing attorney and my attorney, but I needed to prepare myself mentally as well as physically. I wanted to be strong and in a fight mode. I put my red sweater on, black skirt and tall black boots. Somehow that combination made me feel empowered.

That morning I walked into the building where this very prominent law firm was located, we took the elevator to the 36th floor, and it seemed to take forever. Upon arriving, we were directed to a conference room. I have never been in a conference room this big with a huge table that could seat 20 people, and big glass floor to ceiling windows. I just looked at my attorney, who was a good friend who took this case as a gesture of goodwill, not knowing it would evolve into a year and half long case. The sad thing was that I knew and believed the law was on my side, and I hadn't done anything wrong except trust someone who I thought I could, and at the time had no reason not to. She was kind, cheerful, positive and had love for all the same things I did. Believing this, I didn't have her sign a contract. Lesson learned, and after many years of working together and helping her to establish a brand, and a following from my client base, she chose to stab me in the back, taking advantage of an opportunity. So that morning, I had not really been prepared much by my attorney, as we didn't feel like there was much to prepare. I spent seven grueling hours being deposed in this huge conference room by a very experienced opposing attorney. The opposing side constantly rolled their eyes, and made faces, while I was being asked trick questions, using legal terminology I had never heard before. The court reporter typing up all the questions and answers was fascinating—I never saw anyone type so fast! I have to say, it was a very traumatic experience to say the least. In fact, I learned that the truth doesn't really matter much, it was more about how experienced the attorney is when asking questions and trying to trick you into your answers. As always, I would answer everything honestly and truthfully, and in the end of the seven hours, I was completely drained, exhausted, and overwhelmed.

It definitely reconfirmed that I would never want to do anything wrong, untruthful, or illegal. I cannot even imagine being in the same situation again and trying to hide something or make up something.

In the end, we were able to settle this matter out of court the day before trial. There were many more intense meetings and more powerful attorneys, as this case grew into something much bigger than we originally thought. There were mediations which again were more about who had the most money and the best legal connections. I was feeling defeated, I worked so hard, building my business, helping others, and here I was. Even though I knew that the law and the truth was on my side, I was made to feel like I did something wrong and needed to be defending myself.

I have to say, this experience definitely took a great toll on me. I was exhausted, emotionally drained and the amount of stress from simply running a business, plus a great financial loss because someone else decided to steal from my business, plus the stress of fighting this legal matter, plus spending 20 plus hours a week building our case for many months, plus trying to learn all this legal terminology—it was all a lot for this Czech-American girl to handle. I felt like I became an investigator, diving through emails and evidence that was coming at me through all the discoveries and the depositions. It really was heartbreaking and felt like a really ugly divorce where your mean, soon-to-be ex was living happily with his new family right next door to you.

After this matter was over, I have to say it took me a few years to come to terms and make peace within myself regarding it all. Since that experience, I have a little bit of PTSD, I would say, anytime I see a trial or deposition in a movie or on TV. All I can think is, "Will the truth prevail, or will it be a matter of who has deeper pockets, stronger connections, and who is better at asking trick questions?"

And of course, the first lesson learned from this is always make sure you have agreements in writing with contracts signed no matter who you are talking to. Also, don't think that everyone will be stepping into agreements with honesty and pure motives even if it seems like their intentions are honorable at first. Unfortunately, this experience also forced me to modify my personal philosophy about life and business. I'm a little more careful now and people don't really surprise me anymore, although they do still disappoint me at times. And I guess it's human nature that when there is an opportunity, greed can often be stronger than the desire to do what is right. That was a hard lesson to learn.

The second lesson learned in all of this is: make sure you leave time for fishing. Not only is it a wonderful way to relax and unwind, but on many occasions while fishing, I've gotten such clarity when I needed it and also had the opportunity to reset my perspective.

I remember one morning in particular, Gary and I were out on our boat fishing while the sun was just starting to rise and the water was still calm. We were not really that determined to catch anything, although it is always nice. Who doesn't like fresh fish? But that day, we were just happy to be out enjoying the early morning. Several boats were out, and we were sipping our morning coffee, relaxing and drifting, enjoying nature and the sound of nothing. All of a sudden, a big wave came out of nowhere crashing against the side of boat. Our coffee spilled and our fishing lines became tangled. What just happened? And then we saw it. A big tanker in the distance must have created this wave, and at that moment, I realized fishing and business have a lot in common. I know, a little strange, but I realized, just like in business, you never want to lose focus. You have to focus on where you are heading and focus on your surroundings. From then on, I started to share this analogy with our managers, or whenever onboarding a new staff member. I tell them, "You are the captain of the ship, and what that means is that you need to make sure that your ship has all the provisions, all the supplies, all the sailors (team), and know what direction you are heading, in order to have a safe and a successful journey. That means that you need to be prepared for the storms, for the weather changes, the possible mechanical failures, make sure the sailors stay motivated, and be prepared for the possible loss of communication and navigation." That fishing experience also told me that you always want to be alert, vigilant, and aware of your surroundings. Don't ever just let things go completely. You can still enjoy the ride, and relax, but never lose your sense of awareness, or you just might lose more than your coffee.

That same morning of the unexpected wave, we just about finished when we saw a flock of birds circling and diving in an area not too far from us. We reeled our fishing lines back into the boat, and started heading that way, but not too fast. We didn't want to create a distraction, but we also wanted to go fast enough to get there ASAP and not miss the action. The water at that point was bubbling like crazy with fish! It was an incredible experience; we call it our national geographic experience. The water was literally alive with hundreds of mackerel going after bait fish and the birds were going crazy. What a site it was, and we were right in the middle of it! Did we catch any fish? Yes, we sure did. It was a powerful and unforgettable experience that morning.

Even Gary, who is a very experienced fisherman, was beyond excited. What we observed was very rare—a school of migrating mackerel feeding. Although that event lasted only a few minutes, the experience and the excitement of it will last a lifetime.

My business lesson in this was to always be alert, and always be looking out for the next opportunity. You never know when you will hit the jackpot!

So, after our little morning excursion, which was blessed with this little bit of excitement, we headed back to our friend's house where we were staying. Which reminds me of another lesson I have learned in all of this: make sure you always take good care of the friends you have, and they just might let you stay and enjoy their weekend home!

CHAPTER ELEVEN

Longing

The other day, I was at the Motherhood Center when a lady came in and asked who handles the utilities for our building. I explained that it was our landlord's responsibility and she proceeded with some small talk. Then she asked me a common question. She said, "So do you have any children?" I smiled and responded, "Not yet, but in a way I feel like I have thousands of babies through the Motherhood Center."

After she left, I stopped and thought a minute. I had been having the same response now for probably 15 years. I say, "not yet" but the truth is that I'm unable to have children.

When I started my business, I was very focused on building the business, and of course being in the pregnancy and baby industry, I have been surrounded by my clients and their growing families pretty much from the time I arrived in America. I was so focused on growing my business that I was not really focused on building my own family.

My husband and I would work hard and play hard, we traveled a lot. And as years started to roll by, I started to get closer to advanced maternal age. So, when I was in my early thirties, I started thinking about it a little bit more seriously, and I started having this picture in my mind. I love marketing, and I'm always thinking about how I can support and I grow my business. In my mind, I envisioned that I was going to be this expecting business owner. I love pregnant bodies, I think pregnancy is so beautiful and I could not wait at that point to spin out some great marketing—the founder of the Motherhood Center is expecting. I could imagine this photo of me with my bump on a magazine cover.

But as a busy professional, I lost track of the years, and all of the sudden I realized that the pregnancy never happened, and I needed to start looking at things a little bit more seriously. I had some fertility tests done, and long story short, there was 0.02% chance of me getting pregnant. That's not a very good chance. I waited a little longer to start having some more serious thoughts and conversations with Gary, and looking back I guess somehow, I was in denial. How could this be? I love pregnancy, I love babies. How would I not be able to experience the joy of motherhood personally? I had been a part of thousands of pregnancies by that point. Why not my own?

A couple of more years went by and I recognized that I needed to stop being in denial and stop telling myself that pregnancy would just happen. Gary and I needed to have a serious conversation, and since I felt like I was completely lost between what I wanted and what was actually real, so I decided to speak with a therapist to help me process it all. I knew that if I was not at peace with this information it would be difficult to stay in the business I am in.

It is not easy to be wanting to be pregnant and at the same time seeing so many newly pregnant clients on a daily, and really on an hourly basis. I needed to be there for them, and I needed to be there for myself as well.

In recent years, I had some digestive issues, partially stress-induced, and I experienced some extreme bloating. I found myself having fake pregnancy belly from my digestive issues. I know it seems a little odd, but honestly there was a time that I thought maybe I was having a pseudo pregnancy. I actually have a couple pictures of myself looking like I'm about five to six months pregnant. I know this might sound really strange, but I treasure those photographs I actually took, posing as pregnant, as they help me to feel just a little bit closer to my dream.

I have been pretending to be a pregnant lady since my little sister and I role played as children. I would stuff my shirt with a pillow, and put a scarf on my head pretending I had long hair, wobbling through our living room. For me, the thought of not being pregnant or not being able to be pregnant was pretty surreal.

Fast forward, after some counseling sessions, and many tears shed and conversations with Gary and my family, I came to peace with the fact that a real pregnancy and biological children are simply not in the cards for me.

We never know what kind of obstacles we will experience in our life, but it's always important to look at the bigger picture, and whatever our decision is going to be, it needs to feel right, so we don't have any regrets later on.

As I'm writing this story, I have not come up with a good answer yet, as I'm not wanting to tell every person who asks that I'm unable to have children. I know that makes them feel badly for asking. I guess I need to think about it a little bit more and come up with a new answer.

For now, being in the pregnancy and baby business, most people assume that I have children. I am grateful to have two stepsons and now two granddaughters who have given me my grandma name which is Babi.

I read somewhere that "Home is where the heart is." I must say that I definitely have my heart in a few places. I have my heart in my business and a heart for family. And I have three geographical "homes." The first being my hometown in the Czech Republic; second, being Houston and third, my home in Port Aransas located on Mustang island. Home doesn't always need to be a place where you live or spend a lot of time, it really can be any place where you have a sense of comfort, a sense of belonging.

Home is a place where you feel comfortable, a place where you feel loved, and a place where you feel secure. Even if I know I will have a busy and possibly stressful day, it brings me a lot of comfort knowing I will be coming home. I will put on my cozy shirt and sweatpants and enjoy a cup of tea or a wine or beer (Czech girls likes a good beer) and have a home-cooked meal in the company of my loved ones. I have never thought about the meaning of home but lately I have, and there are a few reasons for it. As I'm getting older and wiser (ha-ha), the things I appreciate most are evolving. Although my first home is thousands of miles away, I have a great appreciation that I'm able to visit my homeland of Czech Republic, at least once a year and spend some quality time with my family. Most of the year I spend in my second home, Houston, Texas, where I have been living now half of my life.

Interestingly, I tried very hard to create a one-of-a-kind business. I founded and built a company which ironically, is often referred to as my client's home away from home. Many of my clients are transplants, like me from other countries and other cities, or other continents. I am grateful to give them a home away from home. It's so important to have a good foundation when starting a family. Somehow the words home and family parallel with each other.

Recently I have been following social media messages of my former clients and now a friend is opening my eyes and heart to a whole new level of the meaning of home. She has been working with the homeless population and just thinking about it hurts—a whole population of people without a place to belong. I'm very family-orientated and have a very strong sense of home. Growing up I called many of my neighbors "uncles and aunts" and I know that if I need something, everyone is there to help. There is a great sense of security and a lot of comfort that comes with it. My home life was pretty simple but that's also what was comforting. On the other hand, my second home is in the big city—the fourth largest city in America. You can feel the energy all around, even at three in the morning. You can get access to pretty much anything you want or need at any time of the day or night, any day of the week! I love both of my worlds. I do have to say because of my upbringing even if it was in a different country, it helped me appreciate my life here in America that much more. The access, the freedom, the opportunity. At the same time, I love being able to connect back to my roots, it recharges me, and helps me to bring things back into perspective. It's important that we bring attention to the small things, the sincere smiles, gardening, exploring nature, walking, the appreciation of home cooked meals, family gatherings, grilling, picking fresh veggies and fruits. We can't just let life go by, we must really step out and live it. If you are doing something you don't like, change it. If you don't have people around you who elevate you and support you, change it. You can adjust, change every day, every hour, every minute of your life. The opportunities are out there, you just need to slow down enough to see them and reach for them, and then accept them.

Recently, I went to a conference and they asked us to close our eyes and imagine the place where we feel relaxed, secure, safe. My immediate thought wasn't to some wonderful exotic place I visited. It wasn't the vast ocean or a majestic mountain. My very first thought took me to our kitchen table growing up. We didn't have money for lavish vacations or anything extra for that matter, but I was content. I saw my parents working hard to make sure we had all we needed and they gave my sister and I so much more than money could buy. They gave us care, they gave us love, and made sure we had food on the table. My parents still have that same kitchen table 40 years later and every time I see it or think about it, I am reminded of what home really is.

I've talked about my third home, Port Aransas, located in the South part of the great state of Texas. It was once a small fishing village and is now a mix of local fishermen and small businesses, peppered with tourists coming for weekends or holidays. The snowbirds spend the winter here away from the freezing North. And then there are locals, gifted artists creating beautiful pottery, paintings, and abstracts, creative art and sculptures from driftwood. (Don't worry about those who might be missing a few teeth or living in a dilapidated trailer.) But you'll also see, birdwatchers looking to find unique species, fishermen on airboats, kayaks scouting the shallow flats. Offshore you'll see deep-sea sport fishing boats, sailboats, and yachts. On shore, the village is full of great restaurants and there are many chefs moving to Port Aransas from large cities to share their great culinary talents.

The music scene, just like the art scene, is very diverse. You'll find everything from honky-tonks to Texas rock and roll and pop music all blaring from dance halls.

Then there's the Tarpon Inn historical hotel where President Roosevelt stayed. You can enjoy year around fishing tournaments, the Christmas boat parade, fourth of July fireworks, and beautiful beaches with large sand dunes and an annual Sandcastle Festival.

I've been going to Port Aransas for the last 20 years, it was actually one of my first trips after I arrived here as an au pair. Gary has a few friends who have homes on the island and would invite us there for the weekends.

Port Aransas was where I first experienced wave runners. What a fun toy! I have to say 20-25 minutes on a jet ski is probably all I can take, but one of the most memorable experiences was when my sister visited, and we stopped to watch dolphins. Port Aransas has a lot of dolphins in the channel and around boats, so it's not uncommon to see them but this time we were particularly close. My sister and I were just sitting on our wave runners, resting just about eight feet apart, when all of a sudden the dolphins starting to show off right in front of us. They swam underneath us and popped up on the other side of us. We sat there smiling ear to ear, as this was something we'd never experience in Czech Republic! It was such a neat experience, being a part of their play and so special to have been there with my sister! We stayed there for a little while longer, not wanting it to let go of this precious moment.

Another time, Gary and I decided to head out on our jet skis away from the jetties near the shore to deeper water in the Gulf of Mexico. It was probably my third time on a jet ski, and I was starting to feel fairly confident, but as we approached the deeper waters the waves were becoming bigger and higher. I started to feel a little uneasy. Of course, as you are going through these big waves, it's not easy to talk to someone, so I had no option but to just follow Gary who is a much more experienced jet ski rider. It was quite a scary and exhilarating time.

I realized I had come a long way from my fear of the water in my younger years. Facing fear is the only way to see the growth within us. We can't ever take our life experiences for granted. Oftentimes, the negative experiences allow us to get to the rawness of our feelings and help us to know, see and decide where we want to be in life, and what our priorities are, what we want from life, and who we want to have in our lives.

CHAPTER TWELVE

Til Shellfish Do Us Part

In Czech Republic, our diet and produce is completely different from America. Growing up in Czech Republic, the food was mostly homegrown and very little in the store had additives or preservatives. It's was all very fresh. Even our mayonnaise would be found in the refrigerator section in the grocery store. When I arrived in the states, I experienced all new flavors and tastes. Once Gary and I started dating, we would often go to different restaurants and I was introduced to many foods I never had before or even knew existed. One of them being all kinds of fish and shellfish which was not accessible to us in Czech Republic. Growing up I would eat fresh caught mountain trout or carp on special occasions such as Christmas dinner, but most definitely no ocean fish. Once I discovered shellfish, I was hooked. I would enjoy oysters Rockefeller, Lobster tail, crab cocktails, but my most favorite was shrimp. I absolutely loved shrimp! Since Gary and I would often go to the coast, I would eat fresh shellfish as much as I could. One weekend we were visiting some friends in South Padre Island, a cute beach town with outdoor music. I had been living in Texas about a year and a half. We had dinner in a nearby restaurant and I ordered one of my favorites, Oyster Rockefeller. After dinner, we went to listen to some live music. As the band started to play, we headed to the bar to get a cocktail. As we were standing at the bar, I started to feel light-headed. I thought maybe I had low blood sugar, so I turned to Gary to ask him to order me a sweet drink. But before I got a word out, I fainted and fell to the floor. Of course, no one knew what was happening and a crowd gathered around me. I was unconscious for a couple minutes, and when I opened my eyes, Gary and our friend Glenn were leaning over me and holding my hand. I know everyone was shocked and had no idea what was happening. I had no idea either, I just knew that I needed to step away from the crowds. Many people thought that I was drunk and had just passed out, but I knew I had only had one drink with dinner. Since the band who was playing was friends of my husband, we were quickly escorted to the VIP private area so I could get some rest. As we were walking up the stairs, I started violently throwing up. One of the security men looked at Gary and asked if I had an oyster allergy. He said he wasn't aware of it but I did eat oysters that night. Interestingly enough, the security guard explained there is a specific smell of the vomit which is very specific to oyster or shellfish allergy. He himself developed it later in life after living on the island.

That night, I just rested on the tour bus. This experience was quite frightening, as I felt like I almost died and while I didn't enjoy my body helping me expel what was not good for me, I was grateful. Of course, I did not want to take a chance or risk my life again and decided that I might just need to stop eating shellfish.

A couple of years later, Gary and I were vacationing in Cozumel, a beautiful little island off the coast of Mexico, where there is an abundance of fish and shellfish. One night, we were sitting on the beach enjoying the beautiful sunset and decided to order some conch shell ceviche. I love ceviche. The lime mixed with chopped up peppers and fish combined with beach and sunset and palm trees, and the beautiful ocean—it doesn't get much better. As we wrapped up our evening on the beach, we headed to our hotel to start getting ready to go to dinner. I shared with Gary that I might just want to take a little nap, I was feeling like I need to rest for a bit. After about 20 minutes, Gary was unable to really wake me up. I fell into such a deep sleep that he ended up just ordering room service for himself. Later that night, I woke up, and started violently getting sick for about two or three hours. My body was expelling everything possible, very much like the experience I had the first time around when I had the shellfish allergy. Later on, I learned that conch shell is in the shellfish category, which I didn't realize. Clearly it was not something my body agreed with. At that point, I felt like it was pretty much confirmed that this Czech girl was not meant to be eating oysters, shrimp, or crab meat ever again.

I was of course very upset and sad by this realization. I did feel like at this point, I really needed to have it confirmed by the doctor, which I did, and got confirmation that I have an allergy, and basically my throat closes and heart stops when I eat shellfish. He did strongly suggest for me to carry an EpiPen with me at all times, and next time if I have an allergic reaction I might not wake up from it. His admonition was frightening as I learned how close I was to being gone forever.

A couple of years after that, we were visiting with our friends in Port Aransas by the ocean. Gary cooked two separate meals, one safely prepared for me, and one filled with shrimp for everyone else. After dinner, we all went to enjoy some live music, at a nearby outdoor venue. As we were listening to the music and enjoying a cocktail, I shared with my husband that I'm feeling a little light-headed, that I just needed to step outside to get some fresh air, although we were outside already. As soon as I stepped outside the venue, I saw a little bench, and decided that I was going to rest there for a little bit, but I soon realized I never made it there. Just after stepping outside, I lost consciousness and when I woke up and opened my eyes, all I could see was the asphalt and blood all over my white shirt. I realized that I must have fainted, and as I was trying to get up I was in shock and not really realizing what was happening. I was trying to wave down some incoming patrons, but everyone thought that I was just drunk and tried to avoid me. Finally, an older couple came by and I shared with them that I'm not drunk, that something happened and I need them to help me find my husband. As my husband described the story, he could see this lady walking through the front door, and based on the description I shared with her, she went straight to my husband and asked him if his name is Gary. He jumped up and ran outside to help me. What we realized a little later on, was that there was cross contamination. Our friend accidentally touched my dish with the spoon which had touched the shellfish meal. I realized how sensitive my body is when such a little contamination can stop my breathing.

On that trip, we stayed a little longer before returning back to Houston. My face and arms were scratched up and my nose semi-broken, from the impact when I hit the ground.

With all the near-death experiences at a fairly young age, it really helped shape my perspective on life. I had a few more situations where I was not sure if I was exposed to the shellfish, and started to have little signs of allergy, and to be honest with you, I wrote at least two "goodbye letters" before age 35. The letters were to my loved ones, my husband, and my family in the Czech Republic, sharing how grateful I was for them and the experiences in my life. I wanted to make sure to leave a token of my love for my family and friends.

I would encourage everyone, whenever you are in either a difficult situation, or even during very happy times in your life, to pause, and write down all the things you are grateful for. Acknowledge the things you appreciate and the things which are meaningful to you. Also do not ever hesitate to share verbally with your loved ones, friends, family and associates how much they mean to you, before it might be too late.

CHAPTER THIRTEEN

Finding a Rhythm

It's no secret that sometimes we do things in self-preservation. Preservation of our vulnerability, preservation of our bodies, preservation of our thoughts—something I was experiencing early on. It was so hard to think about my family and my life back in Czech Republic. So, in self-preservation, I poured myself completely into the American culture. Over the years, although I was not able to, or not wanting to, or was simply too busy to have pictures of my family in our house, the memories were still ingrained in my everyday life. Every time I would be washing dishes with a dish rag from Czech my mom gave me, cutting fruits or veggies on my cutting board my dad made, opening up my computer and the password was related to my dad, the towel from my mom I would hang over my shoulder, the sweatpants I would be wearing from my sister, those older treasures and memories are things which keep me in touch with my "history" and precious childhood memories.

I have many little pieces of Czech memorabilia sprinkled throughout the house, but anytime I would be thinking too much about my family back home, tears would start rolling out of my eyes, and I would always try to push them back and start thinking about something else. I trained myself for self-preservation and decided not to think too much about my family and friends back home because it hurts too much. I needed to separate my life, my life before and my life now.

One of the hardest things about writing this book was reaching out to my family members and asking questions about the past. On one hand, I was very excited and curious to learn since we never talked much about it before, but at the same time I had so much reservation about reopening wounds or making people uncomfortable. Maybe not everyone felt the same way about it. So as much as I wanted to validate my feelings and experiences, I was afraid that they will not be aligned with what others experienced. I guess in a way, imposter syndrome was hitting hard during those times.

When the shutdown first happened in 2020, I had the opportunity to spend a few weeks in nature where there were no other people for miles. Gary and I, and our friend, were surrounded by ocean, palm trees, ranch land, and wildlife. One day, a tune came strongly to mind, a melody I had been humming since I arrived to America. Anytime I would go through hard times, this melody would come to my mind. And if I was where no one could hear me, like in the shower, I would start humming this song. It's amazing how music can be so grounding. This song helped center me every time. I had a daily routine where I would get into the golf cart and drive up to the ocean where no one could hear me, and I would start humming the melody louder and louder. One day, I found the courage to start actually singing the words:

Vzhuru na palubu, dalky volaji,
vitr uz prihodny vane nam.
Tajemne pribehy nas ted cekaji,
tvym domovem bude ocean.
V rahnovi plachty vitr nadouva, zene lod v sirou
dal, koleba boky plachetnice,
jak by s ni jenom hral.

The song doesn't translate to English very well but it is basically a song about a group of friends going on a sailboat adventure. They had never been sailing before so the song is describing their awe and wonder at the wind in the sails, the beauty of the sunsets and sunrises, and looking to the horizon for the next adventure.

It was the theme song from a television show I used to watch growing up, so not only did the message of the song ring true to the feeling of my own life's adventures, but it had sentimental meaning as well.

After about two weeks, I was able to fully express my voice, and eventually created a recording of me singing it. It was incredibly freeing, and I was able to express my song to the world—even it was just the birds, deer, fish, quail, or turkey hearing me.

After about four weeks of singing this song every day, I became very comfortable, and at one point, I didn't realize that anyone else could hear me. As I was driving my golf cart back towards the terrace, I saw that Gary and one of our friends were sitting there and they could hear me sing.

My first reaction was complete embarrassment, but this moment lasted just a split-second, and I was able to embrace and move beyond that feeling. It was incredibly freeing, and I felt like I was able to go full circle on my journey and to let my voice be heard.

You see, when I was just a little girl, I was visiting my grandma who I loved so much. One of her friends came over to visit and asked me if I would sing a for them.

Before I could say anything, my grandma, said, "Oh she does not know how to sing." That memory is very strong and was very strong for a long time. Fast forward two years later to my elementary school years, we had music lessons as part of our curriculum. During one of the lessons, our teacher asked one of the students to sing a song. When he started out, he was a little bit off tune, and my friend and I started to giggle. I know it was not the right thing to do, and of course the teacher noticed it, so she asked for me to stand up and sing, which was one of the worst feelings I had. I was so embarrassed that I was first of all making fun of someone else, and now completely embarrassed because I would have to sing in front of the whole classroom. I got up and I wasn't able to make a peep. I was completely voiceless.

Fast forward to my teenage years after the fall, I perfected my lip-syncing capabilities. My friends were so impressed thinking I knew all the new American songs that came to us in English, but really, I was hiding my voice.

One of the many privileges we have in today's world is that we have so many choices and options. It's very important when making decisions to do so from a grounded standpoint. We have to be careful that we aren't making decisions based on emotions, triggered by associations from the past. I like to do things that support grounding and centering every day, throughout the day. It's not always easy, but once you get in the habit of doing so, it's easier to recenter yourself throughout the day as needed.

In the recent months, I was making a point of doing meditation every morning, and sometimes it's just a few minutes, but it's important to really give yourself that time. Meditation doesn't need to be in any special place. Just recently, I had the experience of meditating with the wind blowing in my face, and rays of sunshine tickling my face. I was grateful. But I'm not always able to meditate in nature or in a special place. Sometimes you might find that there is just a little corner in the house where you can meditate and that's good enough. In a way it really doesn't matter what's around you, it matters what's on the inside and being able to recognize that is a great practice. They say meditation is like a muscle, if you exercise it regularly, it can grow, and it will allow you to relax and find a place of calm more quickly.

A few years ago, I attended a charitable event called Books Between Kids, which focuses on literacy and education for children through books. They had a young woman as the keynote speaker, and she shared a story of a child, who grew up in an unhealthy environment, with poverty and abuse. It was assumed that her family members would end up in jail or killed at some point in life. One day, this child was introduced to a book and as she started reading it, it allowed her to escape her reality and get into a completely different world. She was able to explore the good, the adventure, the healthy, and over the years, books became a new world for this child. Later on, this child became an adult, and was able to find a great job. In the end of the presentation, we learned that the young school principal standing in front of us was that child from the story. She was able to pass her goodness to other children and help change their lives for the better.

From that day, I could never forget that story. Every time I see a book, it reminds me that books can be someone's escape from their own reality, and what amazing power books have to change people's lives for better.

I believe that life is all about taking chances, if you don't take chances, you will never know if you are headed in the right direction. If you don't take chances, you might not meet the person who can be your partner for rest of your life. If you don't take chances, you might not know if the business deal which looks too good to be true is really the chance of a lifetime. If you don't take chances, you might never experience the excitement of the unknown, and what can be just around the corner to make your life amazing!

The opposite of taking chances is living in complacency. During communism, everyone was treated equally so if you worked harder it didn't matter. You would not earn more money, you would not be able to advance in anyway because everyone was equal. So, the sense of doing better to accomplish more, or succeeding and exceling wasn't nurtured or supported. But I've learned over the years that something in the core of mankind wants to work, to excel, to accomplish and so I'm grateful for the freedoms we have in America and I'm hopeful that people will continue to fight to protect those freedoms.

When I think about America, first I think about how young it is. In fact, the basement in my parent's home is actually much older than America itself. Coming from Europe, the history is so rich, there's so much that happened before America was founded and established. But to the rest of the world, and to me, America represents one thing—freedom.

As a child, there was no concept of the word "freedom." As a child, freedom meant going outside and running in the rain, if your parents would allow you to do that. You enjoyed the freedom to be able to play with your friends or cousins anytime you wanted to.

Freedom could be mean going to the pantry or fridge and getting whatever snack you would want. Freedom could be getting veggies or fruits in your parents' garden and enjoying it.

As we get older, the sense of freedom, or the meaning of freedom gets redefined. You have the freedom to choose whatever school you would like to go to, based on your grades and talents. You can go to whatever concert you would like to go to and listen to whatever type of music you would like. You have the freedom to make money and choose whatever profession you'd like or travel to any country in the world.

Freedom can mean the ability to read whatever books you want to read, watch whatever TV show you would want to watch, or search whatever you want on the internet, or to listen to whatever radio station you want.

Freedom can mean that belief in the universe, God, or whatever you feel like is the higher power. Freedom also means that you can express your beliefs, desires, opinions openly. And the truth is that not everyone in other countries has these freedoms that I just shared with you. The truth is that if communism didn't fall in 1989, when I was just a young teen, I would not have access to the things I just listed. It's hard to even think about it, now that I'm 40 something.

Freedom is something that we need to cherish and fight for. It is very easy for people to have their freedoms stripped away from them. I've seen it happen, and I've seen the consequences. I've seen the differences in the people's behaviors, in cultures, when they do have freedom and when they don't.

The contrast between the way I grew up and my life in America is stark. When I arrived in America, I felt like I had access to pretty much anything I wanted, if I was willing to work hard and put my efforts and energy towards it. This is the land of opportunity, but the fact is, it is up to me to reach for it.

Who knows what my life would be like if I would have stayed in the Czech Republic? I wouldn't have met my husband or started my business. Who knows what my life would be like if communism never fell? I would have grown up my whole life knowing only the communist regime.

With this understanding, I have a much greater appreciation for freedom.

For someone who did not grow up in freedom, the thought that freedom can be taken away because of the hunger for power by other people, is startling. The reality is that it can actually happen and happen really quickly. I will always be outspoken and encourage people not to not take their freedoms for granted.

CHAPTER FOURTEEN

Living in Contentment

Because of my husband's connections and friends and his family's connections, I have been exposed to a lot of great things. Before my business really started taking off, we traveled even more than we travel now. One year I realized that we traveled most weekends of the year. I found that when I was at home, I was feeling like I was on vacation or like I was in a guest house, confused about which kitchen drawer the silverware was in and which way to turn the faucet on for hot water. But I'm so grateful for the opportunities we've had, and I've learned to be content no matter what the circumstance. There are times when I am flying on a friend's fancy private jet to one of the most unique places in the country and being catered to by many staff. There are places I wake up and go have coffee, and someone makes my bed and tends to my every whim all day long. Of course, I feel very honored and grateful to have that experience. I feel pretty comfortable in that type of environment, but on the other hand, there are times when I am in a very different situation the following week, sleeping on a sofa in the rundown trailer house in a South Texas hunting ranch with mouse traps all over the floor. No one is there to help with anything and I have to get up and make coffee and breakfast tacos early in the morning before we go hunting.

There are times when I'm going to a super nice gala, in a beautiful gown, with a diamond bracelet on, feeling pretty as if I am part royalty (although I'm not) and the next moment I'm in my sweatpants which have definitely seen better days, and a comfy t-shirt, eating scrambled eggs with bacon for dinner. I could not imagine being any happier then right there at that moment, watching a Hallmark movie with my husband! (Although, he would like to be watching something else.)

One time, I had a pretty intense week at work, and I was looking forward to being in the Texas Hill Country at our friend's beautiful property with a spring fed lake, tucked in between rocky hills with greenery all around. I was so looking forward to kayaking, fishing, and swimming; and enjoying the many ducks, deer, swans and other wildlife. I also was looking forward to working on my book in a beautiful spot on the giant rocks, right by the waterfalls. It's a very special place. So as soon as we arrived, we made a quick lunch at one of the quaint cabins which was assigned to my husband and I, with rocking chairs on the front porch overlooking the lake, which provided a perfect spot for morning coffee and afternoon cocktails.

When we arrived, I made a couple of business calls, although the internet is very spotty due to the hills surrounding us, and I was ready to head out to the lake. I put my water shoes on, my towel across my shoulder, and grabbed my sunglasses, hat, and writing pad. I was so excited! Walking towards the waterfalls, there is a dam with rocks stacked up that create a walkway. After the dam, you walk up a small hill and down the other side and there you find the waterfalls. I could hardly wait. I noticed that the dam was not overflowing as it normally does but I kept walking. I went up the hill and down the hill and walked up to what was supposed to be waterfalls, but there was no waterfall. Just the little trickle down the rocks that created little puddles just big enough for hundreds of minnows/ fountain dartitis, and little bugs. I was so disappointed. I was very much ready to unwind while listening to the sound of waterfalls and enjoying the scenery while working on my book. When I realized that the waterfall pretty much dried up due to the current drought, I knew I needed to quickly change my perspective and turn it into gratitude. So, I found something to be grateful for. I was grateful that I had experienced the waterfall before when it was alive and flourishing. I was grateful for the precious moments I already had. But I was also grateful knowing that I could go back to see it again. I was appreciative, and it reminded me to live in the present moment and to treasure those moments. Even though I don't hear the waterfall nor see the greenery around it, I have a memory that can take me right to it.

That moment I learned that I could turn my disappointment into gratitude, knowing that is a better way to live life.

I mentioned I had to work hard to overcome a fear of water. When I was a teenager, I was at our local swimming pool. It's where we would spend many summers, playing volleyball, hanging out with friends, sunbathing, and swimming in our local swimming pool. It's where all the youth from the area would hang out. One time, we were all hanging out, being typical teenagers, and there was a boy I liked. Everybody was jumping into the pool from either the diving board or from the sides, and I wanted to participate. Well, it didn't turn out too well. I made total flop jump from the diving board and the boys were laughing, when I finally resurfaced.

From that moment on, I did have a little bit of an issue (big issue) jumping into the water. I did it a few times since then, but most of the time I would have water getting up my nose, and it was not a pleasant experience.

Fast forward about 18 years later, I'm still having issues jumping into the water. One of our dear friends has a really neat, really one-of-a-kind family place, right on the Comal River. The water is pristine and fed from the nearby spring. The temperature is 72 degrees all year round. We would spend many holiday weekends there with our friends and enjoy really great, live honky tonk music. Even Willie Nelson plays there occasionally. It's a really great Czech German town called New Braunfels.

Well, we would go with friends and everyone would jump in the water and I would just belly flop mostly. It was never much fun for me, but I didn't want to spoil the fun. Until one of our recent trips. I finally figured out how to springboard off the right foot. What a difference! No more belly flops! And I heard it's good to exhale when you dive in. That made a huge difference too! I cannot wait to do that on our next trip!

Although I still have a great respect for water, I'm

starting to let go of the fear so I can really enjoy just being in the water and swimming. This fear began when I was just a toddler and almost drowned. I don't even remember it, but it clearly impacted me all these years, compounded by the very embarrassing moment as a teenager. But now, I'm coming into my own and embracing the water and all the goodness it offers.

When I swim, I'm forced to focus on nothing else but my breathing, inhale and exhale. If I forget that, I start choking, and swallowing water. So, swimming is a great way for me to exercise but also helps me to clear my mind and relax.

I have been realizing while working on this book, that there are some experiences from my childhood which affected the way I am now, or the way I was, and I'm learning the reasons behind all of it. I have a unique perspective, not intentionally, where I was able to experience very diverse lives on different continents.

Certainly, growing up in a communist country will have to have an effect on any human being. As I was growing up, I had no awareness that I was learning a lie in school, or what my parents were not telling me, or how my grandparents actually were suffering. I have not been really aware that all of those experiences are not the same in the rest of the world. Being locked in a country with restricted travel, where all of your radio, TV, and media is censored, displaying a made up picture if you will, to portray a certain vision, or unrealistic reality, really messes with your head. But it was also very interesting to observe how different people responded, how everyone's emotions played a role in their decision-making. I have observed people who, pre-Covid, seemed to have it all figured out. But under this stressful new situation, under the circumstances they completely fell apart, and the forgotten triggers from their childhood start resurfacing, and of course there were so many people who completely rose to the occasion, and were able to become the leaders, with a very clear mind and focus.

And as much as I could have been frustrated with some of the reactions which I was not expecting from people around me, I knew I had to be completely respectful of where they are and completely respectful of their current situation. We are all learning to let go in our own unique ways.

CHAPTER FIFTEEN

Becoming a Warrior

As I was learning more about what was happening our country and about how information was being censored, it made it hard to know what to believe, what was true and what was not. I already know, you can be reading something in a magazine, newspaper, or even in a history book or listening to it on the radio, or seeing it on TV but that information could have been completely manipulated to fit a particular narrative.

During these Covid times, I'm sure many people have done some serious soul-searching. I would almost say that every one of us has done so in the last few months. How could you not? Pretty much everything in our lives, the good, bad or ugly, was turned upside down, and any sense of security we had was disrupted, and any sense of freedom effected. Even those little simple things and pleasures we took for granted, all of a sudden they were either taken away, or had to be adjusted. Every business in the world was effected, every employer, employee, entrepreneur, every industry. Everything.

From very early on, when we start learning about Covid-19, as a business owner I immediately turned my energy into "warrior mode." When I say warrior, I mean that I was trying to be a centered warrior. My goal was to be present, fighting for business, my people, my employees and contractors, all of them depending on the success of my business and my performance. I was fighting for our clients who were expecting, or having babies, and the ability to provide services for them and the classes they needed. As you know, you cannot put pregnancy on hold. I also became a warrior for my family, making sure to do whatever I could to make them feel better, to feel supported, to feel guided, and to know that I was there. But I also realized that I had to fight really hard not to let my emotions get in the way of thinking, learning, and critical decision making.

I will be the first person to say that I'm not much of a technology person. But I think in 2020 everyone had to all of the sudden be open to technology. At least open to learn, and willing to try and explore. Otherwise, you would find yourself not able to have a meeting, or a conversation since everything went digital and online.

So, one of the ways I was making sure that I remained centered, and available during Covid times is that I started my day with morning meditation. For me, it was really allowing myself to spend 15 minutes at the beginning of the day, just sitting still, listening to the outside world, the sounds of the birds chirping, the air flowing, and while listening focusing on my breathing, and exhaling any tension which was building up with each day. As I was inhaling, I was welcoming the universe to help me in leadership, I was clearing my mind, and focusing on positivity, and creativity. I was very determined to do this meditation every day, something to keep me sane, during this insanity.

If you think about it, since no one in our lifetime had experienced anything like this before, we all were just trying to do our best with the information we had, amidst enormous chaos and uncertainty. The world was experiencing massive amounts of confusion, trying to process and digest all the information, trying to decide what's true and what's not, trying to decipher possible outside interests with the information some people would be sharing. My instinct and my intuition were critical during this time. I needed to be with myself. I had a really hard time going on Zoom calls or doing much online research at all. It felt like a major distraction for me, something that did not feel good, so I just went with those feelings.

Initially I was feeling guilty, like I should do more, or create more, but I had to get myself to the point that I needed to be okay with the fact that I did my best. I could not push myself any further, because I knew that I needed to preserve my energy. Of course, I didn't know that the situation was not going to last just a few weeks but many, many months. It was also very interesting to observe how different people responded, and how everyone's emotions played such a major role in their decision-making. I observed people who, in normal life, seem to have it all figured out, but when Covid hit, they completely fell apart.

Since I grew up in communism, my experience has influenced my view on money. In communism and socialism, since everyone is equal, you do not see much of a difference between the income levels of your friends, family members and associates. The only people who do stand out because they have more than others, are the people who are higher up in the Communist Party, which would be at the source so to speak. Many people lost their property when communism took over, and with it, their heritage. It was taken away to be shared "for the good" of others. Land and income both were dispersed through the community. My grandparents' grocery store, which they built, owned and operated for many years was taken when communism took over, and they became employees of the government and they were dictated to on how to run their own business. My grandparents were forced to sell their business to the government for a very nominal fee, and when I say nominal fee, something of the value of a fur coat for my grandma.

My other grandparents, on my mom's side were forced to give up their land they had for generations to the communal cause, creating collective farms. They were given no other options. Everything was run by a centralized government. The farmers who would disagree would be prosecuted and imprisoned, so the majority of the landowners and business owners just gave in.

That was after the year 1948, when Czechoslovakia was given to Russia and the country was run this way until the fall of communism in 1989. People had no incentive to do better, and there was no reward, so they lost their drive. Also, since everyone had to have a job, oftentimes there would be three people doing the work of one. If you didn't have a job, you would go to jail. Everyone had the same things, and everyone had to work, doing something.

When communism fell, many people who were at the source and knew that there would be properties given back, were able to purchase them for nearly nothing, many people changed coats, turncoat, basically one day they were big communist supporters and the next days they were anti-communist.

Sometimes I can feel an internal conflict between living in democracy vs living in communism. Since so much of the conversation and information was censored during communism, it was hard to process and understand. Think about it, if you are growing up and the information you are given from the newspaper, TV, radio or even in school is manipulated in a way that makes you believe that this is the right way to live, over time, you might just give in. One might just get tired of being pushed down and facing the possibility of being punished for believing differently. It can be easier to give in when so many forces are going against you. You also don't know how much you are giving up since you aren't allowed to connect with the outside or know what you are missing. You are not allowed to travel or listen to news or radio from other countries that are not communist countries. It's hard to find the truth or learn the truth and most don't know they are living a lie.

Change is good if it creates a better life and better opportunities. But change that brings restriction and oppression is not good. That is what happened in

Czechoslovakia, when it was taken over by the Soviet Union, and communism and socialism imposed on the Czech and Slovak people.

It wasn't always that way. Czech Republic became its own country for the first time in 1918, where prior to that we were under the Habsburg monarchy, and because of the geographical location, and very strategic position in Central Europe, Czech Republic was always under some type of war or trying to being taken over by Turks, Habsburgs, and of course World War 1, World War II, and communism for additional 40 years.

Yes, the Covid situation has triggered a lot of different emotions. Ironically enough, there are many parallels between what is happening in America and what happened in my own country. Watching the freedom of being able to do things taken away, and as a small business owner, I had so many clients and so many employees depending on me, on my decisions, and my creativity. All of the sudden so much was stripped away. In the beginning, even the situation of not having toilet paper brought back the memories of growing up. We would use newspaper, especially at my grandma's house, for toilet paper, and it would be neatly cut up in a little holder, in the restroom. This was quite common, as toilet paper was not cheap and sometimes not easy to get under communism.

One of my most memorable fairy tales growing up was a story about a king and his three daughters which he loved very much. When it was time for him to start thinking about passing the kingdom to one of his daughters, he needed to make the hard decision; which one of his daughters would be the best in this role. After much thinking, he decided to give each one of his daughters a question, about their love for him, their father, the King. And from there he would decide which one of the daughters will take over the kingdom. The oldest daughter shared with her father King that she loves him as much as gold. He was of course very pleased with the answer as gold is very treasured and it shows how much she loves him. The middle daughter was asked the same question, and her answer was diamonds. The King was very pleased with that answer as well as diamonds are also very treasured and that means that she loves her father very much as well. The youngest daughter, probably the most kind and loved by the kingdom, was asked the same question. "How much do you love me, my daughter?". Without much hesitation she passionately shared that she loves him as much as salt. He quickly asked her to repeat her answer as he thought that he misunderstood. She proudly repeated it, "I love you more than salt."

The King was incredibly hurt and disappointed by her answer and he asked her to not only leave the kingdom but also ordered all of the salt from the kingdom to be removed. Just to show her how little she actually really thinks of him. Sometime later after the people of the Kingdom suffered greatly as not having salt was so hard, not only was food not tasting good, but also none of the meat and other foods were able to be stored and preserved so people were getting sick. The whole Kingdom knew about the importance of salt. After much deliberation even the king came to the realization that actually his daughter, his youngest daughter, was the one who loved him the most and salt is priceless. And as most fairy tales have happy endings, this is one had as well. The daughter on her travels throughout the kingdom, helped a struggling older woman. She helped to take care of her during the times she needed the most and in exchange this older woman shared with her a small leather bag of salt she had hidden. The young princess with a good heart started sharing the salt with others in need, when she soon realized that the bag of salt was actually endless, and in the end she was able to replenish the salt throughout the whole kingdom and eventually became the queen of the kingdom.

A few years ago, on one of my trips back home, a

friend shared with us about salt mines in Poland, which is just an hour drive from my hometown. I let my husband know that it might be a fun road trip. We don't generally don't go to many places where we need to stand in a long line for tickets to get in. We ended up waiting in line about an hour for our tickets and we were ready to see why there was such great interest to get into these salt mines. To all of our disbelief, we really had no idea about the enormity of these underground salt mines. We learned that these salt mines were first excavated in the 13th century and produced salt continuously until 2007. These salt mines chambers were about 178 miles (287 km) long and went down to 327 meters, which was nine levels down. We of course didn't see the whole underground, just less than 2% of the salt mine passages. But what we did see was absolutely incredible, handcrafted dozens of statues and four fully salt rock carved chapels, with great dome structures with rock salt chandeliers, also underground lake, and "paintings" which were all carved out of rock salt. We learned more about the importance of salt and how salt was critical for not only the wealth of the kingdoms, but also the well-being of people and how treasured those positions of these salt miners were. Generally, the salt miners and their families were healthier and lived longer than others, there were even horses which grew up in the salt mines which helped with the treadmill mining of the salt to the surface. It was all quite amazing and really changed our perspective on something that we never previously thought too much about. I can't imagine what life would be without salt.

Sometimes the most valuable things in life are the things seen as ordinary or common—until we lose them. Before the year 2020, how many of us took for granted the simple freedoms we enjoyed on a regular basis? Things like the ability to work, to run your business, to speak freely, to go to church, to travel, or to simply give a hug or a smile. Something in me rises up as I consider the events of this last year in light of my upbringing, knowing that these things can be taken away permanently, in an instant. Yes, I have lived half of my life without freedom, and half of with freedom. And while I do not regret either, given a choice it would be no contest. Living with freedom, living the American dream is more than I could have ever imagined. And as I've become a warrior for my family and for my business, and for my loved ones, I have become a warrior for this country that is now my home and for the freedoms I've embraced.

May we never lose sight of the treasure that preserves our hopes and dreams and adds zest and flavor to our lives—the treasure to live and love freely. It is this treasure that has afforded me the most amazing opportunities in this life, not only me but hundreds of millions of others who call America home.

May we never forget where we've come from and never lose the drive and passion to stand up for what we believe in and fight for what we hold dear.

About the Author

Gabriela Gerhart is the founder of the Motherhood Center. She established this haven for mothers in 2000, turning a lifelong dream into reality. Gabriela discovered her passion for babies and childcare at an early age while growing up in a small village in the Czech Republic. She received her degree in Pediatric Nursing and worked in the Pediatric ER before accepting a position in the United States as an au pair. After arriving here she quickly realized that women lacked the village and family aspect of pregnancy and motherhood support. The idea for the Motherhood Center grew out of Gabriela's desire to provide women a resource they can trust. A place where they can access current information, instructional care, and professionals that will cater to their individual situation and needs throughout the adjustment for pregnancy and motherhood. "The Motherhood Center is my way of offering these amazing women not only my expertise, but all the best Houston has to offer the mothers, babies, and the families." Today Gabriela touches the lives of thousands of infants, parents and families through the Motherhood Center in Houston, and virtually all over the country.

Gabriela is recognized as an expert in the field of pregnancy and early-stage child development and has delivered keynote addresses for local and national conferences and women's organizations. She has intimate knowledge of the newborn and childcare care industry as well as massage, yoga, and pregnancy education. She holds committee and board positions on several non-profit organizations around the Houston area, focused on helping women and babies. The simple pleasures in life bring her the most happiness. In her free time she enjoys golfing, reading, quality time spent with family and friends, and traveling with her husband.

Acknowledgments

I would like to thank the following for their
contributions to this project:

Joanna Hunt-Boyer
Book Coaching and Collaboration
www.JoannaKHunt.com

Chris Boyer
Creative Direction, Cover Design and Interior Layout

Anthony Rathbun Photography
Cover Photography

Tatiana Massey
Hair & Make Up

My friends Denise, Karen, Lori, Nichole,
and Tricia, my beta readers who provided wonderful
feedback and encouragement!